The Seven Psychic Paths

The Many Classifications and Archetypes of Psychics and Mediums Beyond Empath Abilities

Aly Cardinalli

ALY CARDINALLI LLC

The Seven Psychic Paths; The Many Classifications and Archetypes of Psychics and Mediums Beyond Empath Abilities © 2025 Aly Cardinalli LLC, Texas, United States

Text © 2025 Aly Cardinalli, First Edition

Cover designed by Aly Cardinalli

Paperback ISBN 979-8-9920110-2-9

e-book ISBN 979-8-9920110-3-6

No portion of this book may be reproduced in any form without written permission from the publisher or author, except as permitted by U.S. copyright law.

This publication is designed to provide accurate and authoritative information in regard to the subject matter covered. It is sold with the understanding that neither the author nor the publisher is engaged in rendering legal, investment, accounting or other professional services. While the publisher and author have used their best efforts in preparing this book, they make no representations or warranties with respect to the accuracy or completeness of the contents of this book and specifically disclaim any implied warranties of merchantability or fitness for a particular purpose. No warranty may be created or extended by sales representatives or written sales materials. The advice and strategies contained herein may not be suitable for your situation. You should consult with a professional when appropriate. Neither the publisher nor the author shall be liable for any loss of proYt or any other commercial damages, including but not limited to special, incidental, consequential, personal, or other damages. All Rights Reserved. No part of this publication may be reproduced or transmitted in any form or by any means, electronic or mechanical, including photocopy, recording or any other information storage and retrieval system, without prior permission in writing from the publisher.

Illustrations by Aly Cardinalli
Be the first to know

www.alycardinalli.com

Contents

1. The Sevens — 3
2. Discovery — 20
3. 1s: Physicians — 26
4. Clairvoyant Physician — 28
5. OS Clairvoyant Physician — 30
6. Clairaudient Physician — 32
7. OS Clairaudient Physician — 34
8. Claircognizant Physician — 36
9. OS Claircognizant Physician — 38
10. Clairsentient Physician — 40
11. OS Clairsentient Physician — 42
12. Clairgustant Physician — 44
13. OS Clairgustant Physician — 46
14. Clairalient Physician — 48
15. OS Clairalient Physician — 50
16. 2s: Luminators — 52
17. Clairvoyant Luminator — 54

18.	OS Clairvoyant Luminator	56
19.	Clairaudient Luminator	58
20.	OS Clairaudient Luminator	60
21.	Claircognizant Luminator	62
22.	OS Claircognizant Luminator	64
23.	Clairsentient Luminator	66
24.	OS Clairsentient Luminator	68
25.	Clairgustant Luminator	70
26.	Os Clairgustant Luminator	72
27.	Clairalient Luminator	74
28.	OS Clairalient Luminator	76
29.	3s: Harrowbinders	78
30.	Clairvoyant Harrowbinder	80
31.	OS Clairvoyant Harrowbinder	82
32.	Clairaudient Harrowbinder	84
33.	OS Clairaudient Harrowbinder	86
34.	Claircognizant Harrowbinder	88
35.	OS Claircognizant Harrowbinder	90
36.	Clairsentient Harrowbinder	92
37.	OS Clairsentient Harrowbinder	94
38.	Clairgustant Harrowbinder	96
39.	OS Clairgustant Harrowbinder	98
40.	Clairalient Harrowbinder	100
41.	OS Clairalient Harrowbinder	102

42.	4s: Echoseers	104
43.	Clairvoyant Echoseer	106
44.	OS Clairvoyant Echoseer	108
45.	Clairaudient Echoseer	110
46.	OS Clairaudient Echoseer	112
47.	Claircognizant Echoseer	114
48.	OS Claircognizant Echoseer	116
49.	Clairsentient Echoseer	118
50.	OS Clairsentient Echoseer	120
51.	Clairgustant Echoseer	122
52.	OS Clairgustant Echoseer	124
53.	Clairalient Echoseer	126
54.	OS Clairalient Echoseer	128
55.	5s: Bondreaders	130
56.	Clairvoyant Bondreader	132
57.	OS Clairvoyant Bondreader	134
58.	Clairaudient Bondreader	136
59.	OS Clairaudient Bondreader	138
60.	Claircognizant Bondreader	140
61.	OS Claircognizant Bondreader	142
62.	Clairsentient Bondreader	144
63.	OS Clairsentient Bondreader	146
64.	Clairgustant Bondreader	148
65.	OS Clairgustant Bondreader	150

66.	Clairalient Bondreader	152
67.	OS Clairalient Bondreader	154
68.	6s: Veritant	156
69.	Clairvoyant Veritant	158
70.	OS Clairvoyant Veritant	160
71.	Clairaudient Veritant	162
72.	OS Clairaudient Veritant	164
73.	Claircognizant Veritant	166
74.	OS Claircognizant Veritant	168
75.	Clairsentient Veritant	170
76.	OS Clairsentient Veritant	172
77.	Clairgustant Veritant	174
78.	OS Clairgustant Veritant	176
79.	Clairalient Veritant	178
80.	OS Clairalient Veritant	180
81.	7s: Lenseborns	182
82.	Clairvoyant Lenseborn	184
83.	OS Clairvoyant Lenseborn	186
84.	Clairaudient Lenseborn	188
85.	OS Clairaudient Lenseborn	190
86.	Claircognizant Lenseborn	192
87.	OS Claircognizant Lenseborn	194
88.	Clairsentient Lenseborn	196
89.	OS Clairsentient Lenseborn	198

90.	Clairgustant Lenseborn	200
91.	OS Clairgustant Lenseborn	202
92.	Clairalient Lenseborn	204
93.	OS Clairalient Lenseborn	206
94.	Precognition	208
95.	Precognitive Physician	209
96.	Precognitive Luminator	210
97.	Precognitive Harrowbinder	211
98.	Precognitive Echoseer	212
99.	Precognitive Bondreader	213
100.	Precognitive Veritant	214
101.	Precognitive Lenseborn	215
102.	How This Affects Mediums	216
103.	Death Mediums	218
104.	Channeler	220
105.	Oracle	222
106.	Prophet	224
107.	Dark Medium	226
108.	Infernal Medium	228
109.	Celestial Medium	230
110.	Pet/Animal Medium	232
111.	Plant Medium	234
112.	Weather Medium	236
113.	Elemental Medium	238

114. Putting It Together and Getting to Know the Author ... 240

Secret Chapter

The Sevens

Once upon a time, tales spun around a fire. Whispered individuals touched by the divine or cursed by their green eyes, curly hair, or birthmark could glimpse the weave of fate, hear the silent murmurs of the heart, or foretell the tumbling dice of destiny. Psychic abilities have dwindled to the fringes of folklore and skepticism in our modern era, and it is extremely rare for anyone to have all or most of these abilities. In the human development and evolution of cognitive progress, psychic abilities, which have been present since the beginning of the development of human spiritual cultures, have ebbed and flowed with popularity or access throughout all continents. The question of our diminished psychic ways comes to mind. Let's explore the genetic, historical, and cultural dimensions that have led to the eradication of acknowledged psychic phenomena in the modern era.

The Spanish Inquisition, cloaked in fear and suspicion, became perilous to exhibit any extraordinary perceptions. The inquisitors hunted those believed to harbor unnatural talents. The genetic predisposition towards psychic abilities faced a bottleneck; its prevalence was sharply erased with fear-induced murder. During this period, fear and suspicion were the only subscriptions permitted, and those with abilities seen as "witchcraft" could guarantee death. The Inquisition led to the suppression or eradication of many who possessed these extraordinary sensory perceptions, which significantly reduced the number of people who could have passed these psychic genes to future generations.

Fast forward to the end of the Inquisition (which ended only in 1834, by the way), psychic abilities' decline was a sociological response to cultural disagreement, akin to the outcome of a child raised in a room free of light. If a child were raised in a room without light, the child's eyes would never learn to see in this environment. Similarly, psychic sensitivities, potentially latent in many of us, are left undeveloped under the heavy judgments of societal norms (shoot, my life is laden with ostracization, stigmatization, and objectification).

From childhood, we are taught to dismiss or rationalize away experiences that fall outside the empirical norms, leaving no room for the juvenile experience of ESP. With enough denial of their experiences, their abilities are muted or deafened.

These fleeting, inexplicable moments, like knowing who's calling before the phone rings or experiencing an unexplained premonition, are often shrugged off or forgotten. Like muscles left unused, these psychic senses atrophy without the light of acknowledgment, practice, and acceptance. Now, we have a populace largely disconnected from these once-integral experiences who view ESP as superstition or the workings of charlatans.

Yet, as with all evolution, whether biological or societal, where we are now is not the final outcome of any species; it is ever-changing. Just as eyes might adjust slowly to diminished light after long darkness, humanity is beginning to sense again.

When I first started training psychics at BearBridge Academy five years ago, I learned that even if two psychics had the same psychic senses, they could find completely different aspects in any situation. For instance, two psychics who are both Clairvoyant can be given the same situation and see completely different parts of the same puzzle. I gave the case of Lizzie Borden to my group of elite psychics, The Psychic Guild, at BearBridge Academy of Witchcraft and Psychic Development. One Clairvoyant saw that Ms. Borden was connected to another woman, who was in the building the day of the murders. Another saw the kitchen and could describe the large windows and long counter, with lots of light coming in, unable to leave this room to see more. Another saw an axe at the bottom of the stairs and could describe the axe and the blood on the ground in extensive detail, unwavering in her conviction of what she saw.

Each psychic saw different aspects, and all the pieces fit together, but there wasn't a lot of overlap. Why?

I mean, listen, the fact that the psychics aren't piggybacking on each other's answers tells me how high the psychics hold their integrity as legitimate psychics at BearBridge Academy. Also, while each one is reading, I'm reading the psychic to help them understand if they miss anything or misinterpret anything. No one is fabricating what they are reading so that they have something to contribute by copying someone else. If a psychic didn't have anything from a reading for a client or for an unsolved case, they simply stated so.

Now, let's look at this: If two psychics who technically have the same senses are looking into the same thing, why can't they experience the same things or access the same information? Let's use someone's love life as an example (since so many of us psychics get asked that question the most). Beth wants to find out about this guy she is dating and why he is being so distant. Psychic Sarah says, "I can tell the relationship is frayed. You said something about his mom that triggered a reaction that had to do with his ex." Beth confirms this.

Psychic Fiona says, "He has a typical dismissive avoidant personality where your views on how to connect are triggering him to run. My personal advice is that this is not your problem to fix. My opinion aside on what to do, I know that he is avoidant and will keep running any time you two interact."

Psychic Carole says, "Beth, when you were seven, your dad brutally beat you... Why do you think I'm being shown this? When it comes to this relationship? Does this violence have to do with your sense of value in relationships?"

Beth replies, "Wow, that's really accurate. I think it's because I tend to stay with men who dominate aspects of my life."

Psychic Willow says, "Beth, you dream of a place where you and a partner can sit on the deck with your spiked iced tea and laugh as you watch the sunset. Is he that guy? Because I see you there, but not with this man."

Beth replies, "That is my fantasy. And I guess not."

Psychic Penny said, "Girl, purple nail polish."

Beth is shocked: "How did you know that?"

Psychic Penny says, "I see it. What's the deal with the purple nail polish?"

Beth says, "That's what the big fight was about, but turned into so many other things."

All of the psychics are accurate, but they don't experience the same items. They are all looking at the same problem and experiencing different aspects with their different psychic strengths. This is why I have created the Seven Psychic Paths.

Difference Between a Psychic and a Medium:

Electromagnetic Energy: The study of psychics in the late 1800s was part of the Spiritism movement. The primary location for this study was Duke University. Ectoplasm was the term for the energy that psychics access and get information from. As with anything genuine, counterfeits soon appeared. False mediums were creating a goo in order to prove that they were psychics or mediums in table-tipping sessions or seances. What is laughable about the fact that people believed this was that prior to the word "ectoplasm," psychics, shamans, faith healers, mediums, and witchdoctors were experiencing spirits without excretions. No goo detected.

Because of this idiotic chaos of goo creating counterfeits, we now have the word "electromagnetic energy." This is an energy ... perhaps an aura or the spirit of a thing that comes off of something. If we suppose that humans have a soul, the unique soul signature of each human is their electromagnetic energy signature.

Animism is the belief that all items have a soul signature. If you read my books, you will know that I strongly believe in animism because psychics can understand information from inanimate objects that have no mental source signature to create information. If we were to say that all items have a soul, then we would call that energetic signature "electromagnetic energy."

How is a psychic doing that? What are you doing? When we see, we are viewing items where light refracts off an object. When we hear, our ears perceive sound waves. Psychics access electromagnetic energy, and their dominant senses process this energy into information for which the mind and nervous system interpret. Eyes read light. Ears read sound waves. Psychics read electromagnetic energy.

Psychic: Accessing electromagnetic energy from the mundane and tangible world. The psychic experience is measurable. We have the ability to measure and affirm the information that the psychic has retrieved (even if it is inconvenient).

For instance, a Clairsentient may have a mark that shows up on their arm in the shape of a pitchfork. We can determine that he is connecting to someone who has that same mark, even if we don't know where or who it is. We find out that he is a gamer and that one of his friends in Poland has that mark from a burn when he was a kid. The Clairsentient was connected to the electromagnetic energy of his friend, and his body recreated the mark.

Or, for instance, a Clairaudient hears in her head a man yelling at his mother about putting the pots and pans in the wrong place. She doesn't know who the man's voice is. It isn't a neighbor because the only neighbor she has in her duplex is a gay couple. The next day, while she is at work, her co-worker's husband drops off lunch, and she recognizes the voice as the one she heard in her head. The Clairaudient walks past her co-worker and husband to overhear that the co-worker has a kitchen organizer rack in the back of her car for her husband to pick up. The Clairaudient was connecting to the electromagnetic energy of her co-worker, overhearing the argument her husband was having in her head the previous night.

Medium: Medium literally means "in-between", "agency to do something," or "intervening impression which communicates to our senses." In other words, a medium accesses electromagnetic information from a non-measurable source, their Clairs process the information, and they relay it to us living people. There are many kinds of mediums, but the most well-known is a death medium. These are the ones who access information from the human dead and relay it to us. We call them a medium because they are the in-between for what is here and what we cannot prove. Can we prove that the information is accurate? Yes. Can we prove who the medium is communicating with? No. Therefore, we cannot prove the source of information, making them an agency intervening between you and something unknown to our provable tools and resources.

We also can't prove the opinions of a plant, what a god has to say, the internal voice of a dog, or if the flickering of the lights is because of an entity (all different mediums). We can prove that the information is accurate, which the medium relays in many situations, but not the source.

The Clairs:

Clairvoyant: Clairvoyance represents the mental capability to visualize events, people, or objects as "clear seeing," and it can appear as visions or dream-like images. A common question regarding Clairvoyant phenomena is how do we know if something is a vision or imagination? My experience in training and having Clairvoyance myself is that imagination is more explicit. Furthermore, once a developed psychic pays attention to the connection of energy, they will notice if what they are seeing is because of being connected to an outside source of energy or if they are creating it from deductive imagination. Is there an energy signature associated with the vision? Is it clear like imagination or daydreaming?

Clairaudient: Clear hearing describes the sense of perceiving sounds, voices, or messages through one's mind. The ability to hear voices and sounds in their mind shows itself through inner voices or auditory impressions and may also resemble music or other sounds. It is interesting to note that hearing voices is no longer the primary diagnostic element for mental illness. Most people hear songs, voices, or arguments in their heads. A Clairaudient gets these sounds from electromagnetic energy input and connection.

Claircognizant: The ability to "know" information without logical reasoning or prior knowledge is "clear knowing." Individuals with this sense experience sudden insights or truths as "intuition." They may just know something. I believe that many more people have Claircognizance than any other sense, and those psychics go unnoticed because the media has a hard time capitalizing on this sense with entertainment. Many empaths are almost Claircogs, but if they open up that "intuition," or instinct, and really connect to energy, they would be Claircognitive psychics.

Clairsentient: Clairsentients possess the ability to feel energies and emotions from others and environments through an ability termed "clear feeling." They can also feel in their body what someone is going through physically as well. Many empaths believe they are Clairsentient, but sadly, are not. A Clairsentient isn't "reacting" to what they perceive. A Clairsentient is reproducing what is happening within someone else. An empath or highly sensitive person reacts to the world around them, but a Clairsentient's body is a sensor for what is happening within someone else or a place.

Clairgustant: The rare ability to anticipate the taste of substances without physical contact, referred to as "clear tasting." This phenomenon is often associated with receiving impressions or messages through flavors. They can also be someone who can tell how something will taste while preparing without actually eating anything. They can put together drinks without having any knowledge of the chemical or taste profiles. They can also know if something is dangerous or poisonous. They may also get tastes in their mouth, have dry lips, or salivate as signs based on the connection to various electromagnetic energies.

Clairalient: The ability to detect scents or odors that are not physically present, also called "clear smelling." They can include the scent of a loved one who has passed or an aroma associated with a memory. They will also know how something smells without smelling it, and they can have aromas come to them (either in thought or in literal smell) that tell them about someone's health, character, or if a situation is safe.

Psychokinetic (or Telekinetic): The ability to influence or move physical objects with the power of the mind. They include manipulating matter or causing motion without physical interaction. Telekinetics are not just moving, but actually taking on an object's weight as if they are physically holding it without using their body. They use *their* energy, rather than reading the energy from others. For instance, if a psychokinetic gets a bowling ball to "levitate," they are actually lifting it. A scale underneath the psychokinetic will register the additional weight of the "floating" ball.

Degrees of Sensitivity

Here, let's discover the degrees of sensitivity that someone can have in each psychic sense.

0-2 Normies:

Everyone has some sort of instinct. These people are the ones making up the majority during the Spanish Inquisition because they hunted everyone who would be a 5 or above (or at least those suspected of being more than a 5: "suffer not a witch to live"). Most of us have gut instincts when something is wrong, don't trust someone whom we are meeting for the first time, or have a sense of fear that we need to listen to before walking into a building. Normies should have the know-with-all to figure out not to say something in a situation (if they aren't situationally inept), and not because they know something is going to happen or that they know it would offend someone (not suspect or deduce; but know). Fun fact: at BearBridge, we call people with no psychic abilities "potatoes," because they are about as psychic as a potato (and just all eyes).

3-5 Intuitive Empath:

These people have instincts and are affected by energies. We can even call them Highly Sensitive Persons or HSPs, which the American Psychological Association now recognizes. That means that more and more people identify as sensitive to their reactions to world events, family situations, work environments, cultural or societal norms, and even weather or planetary changes. Empaths are known to be highly observant, intuitive, thoughtful, conscientious, and creative. Many employers consider empaths and highly sensitive people top contributors because of their sensory processing sensitivities.

Many people identify with the term empath, for which they are not. They are much more affected and in tune, and should be identified as psychics.

Empaths will not be able to identify their psychic archetype because they lack the accuracy to really understand what kinds of information they can access.

Now, personally, I don't like the term empath. Most people are empathetic (at least you would hope). Empathy is simply having an affinity for or reaction to something that happens around you. We should all be empathetic and have the ability to react and feel those emotions, but if those emotions aren't tied to someone's intuition, then they are not actually empaths. Some empaths are psychics. I hope they stop using the term "Empath," and start using the terms I hand you in this book. You are more than an Empath.

9-6 Psychic:

This is someone highly sensitive in any of the Clairs above, which can flex and adjust daily between a 6 and a 9. These are "psychics," able to consistently repeat outcomes of accessing information with their Clairs and without the need for their physical senses. During the Spiritism movement and at the Duke University study of psychics, a psychic only needed to be more than 25% accurate when tested for their Clairvoyant abilities in order to be a "psychic." I disagree with this. Someone should not call themselves psychic unless they are more than 70% accurate when relaying anything psychic, including any of the psychic senses listed above. If they are less than 60%, then we would put them in the intuitive category and not the psychic category. Real psychics, in the various senses and archetypes (coming!), are more than 70% consistently accurate.

The regular psychic is not suspecting or deducing. They are accurate without being given information.

10 Over Sensitive (OS):

This is an Over Sensitive. In order to describe what an OS is, we have to introduce synesthesia. Synesthesia is a fancy name for when you experience one of your senses through another. The synapses in someone's brain are crossed regarding abstract thought, so the perception of one item is mixed with another.

For example, you might hear the name "Alex" and see green in your mind. Or you might read the word "street" and taste citrus fruit. The condition occurs from increased communication between sensory regions and is involuntary, automatic, and stable over time.

So, OS Clairvoyant's signals are mixed. The signals they get from electromagnetic energy and the signals their brain receives from their eyes viewing light's refraction off of items get mixed in their head. The brain is mixing up psychically and visually accessed information, presenting them both in the mind of the OS as both being ocular. The psychic's experience is that what they see in front of them is something that should only be in their mind, and they are unable to tell the difference between what is psychic and what is physical.

Simply, an OS Clairvoyant death medium cannot tell the difference between a living person standing in front of them and a dead one (like the show, *Ghost Whisperer*).

OS Clairvoyant: Can't tell the difference between what they see in front of them and what is in their mind psychically; it comes across as hallucinations.

OS Clairaudient: They can't tell the difference between what they hear in the world around them, caused by sound waves, and what they access psychically. They are not actually hearing voices with their ears because no sound waves are being created, but their mind mixes the signals of psychic and auditory input.

OS Claircognizant: Geniuses. A genius is an individual who exhibits exceptional intellectual or creative power. Geniuses skip the structured process of acquiring knowledge or skills through systematic instruction, study, and practice. Geniuses bypass some or all of the structured stages of "introduce, discover, fail, relearn, teach," and display an intuitive grasp of complex subjects they were not exposed to.

OS Clairsentient: Stigmata. This can appear as symptoms of DID, like how one personality has diabetes or green eyes and the other personality doesn't, except that the personalities are all one and the same. The body is just changing based on who the psychic is connected to. The psychic's body's nervous system mirrors identically the reaction to something actually happening to the person they are connected to (like having the symptoms of a heart attack but nothing wrong with the heart or bleeding with a puncture wound). This can also look like Bipolar Disorder because the emotions come from nowhere; however, if they are actively able to prove that it is mirroring someone else (nearby or a social connection of some sort), then it isn't bipolar, but psychic instead.

OS Clairgustant: Someone who can't tell the difference between real tastes and what happens to them psychically (this would ruin me as a person; just give me a lobotomy).

OS Clairalient: Someone who can't tell the difference between smells that are happening and the knowledge of smells they receive psychically.

Bleeds/Triggers:

This refers to an area or set of events that <u>cause</u> psychics to get information. So far, you've learned about the senses, the difference between psychics and mediums, and the level of sensitivity for psychics. We also need to understand that what triggers a psychic can range from person to person.

Many psychics receive information from electromagnetic energy that is around them by proximity or are connected to the auric field because of connections that they have with a place, person, or object. In other words, just by being in the room with something, most psychics can connect to the energy and "read" it. Another way of reading is when a psychic is connected to someone. Do you know how a "cord-cutting" is supposed to end the connection you would have to someone or someplace? Well, psychics can read through those connections without needing to be in the same room.

When a psychic isn't connected to something they need to read, they may need a trigger or a bleed. A trigger is something that jump-starts the psychic, like divination tools, where they point and act as a filter to get the psychic there. A bleed is something where a psychic has one thing happen, and it bleeds into their other senses. For the sake of simplicity, we will combine them here. I won't be placing all of the different kinds of divination techniques because that would be its own book.

Psychometry (also known as Clairtagence) refers to a trigger in which physical contact helps establish a connection between electromagnetic energy and the psychic's perception or insights. For instance, if I had a missing person's case, a policeman could give me something of the person's and I would use that to connect to her. Or if I'm in a dance club, I can shake someone's hand or touch their shoulder to determine their deepest desires (oh yeah, we can do that, because I'm a Clairtagent Claircognitive Harrowbinder).

Oneirognosis/Dreams: The ancient Egyptians believed that while you were in a dream state, you could receive messages from the gods, and many believe they receive messages from the dead. This is called Oneiromancy. If, for instance, this were the case in visions, someone who was receiving messages from the gods in their dream would be an Oneirognosis Clairvoyant Oracle Medium. If a dreamer were talking to the dead and getting auditory messages, she would be an Oneirognosis Clairaudient Death Medium. And if the information were only about the relationship the dead had to someone, they would be a Oneirognosis Cliaraudient Bondreader Death Medium.

Precognition: Although precognition means knowing the future, it isn't a "cog" thing. I mean that having access to the future doesn't automatically make someone Claircognitive. It's a future access thing. So, although it has "cognitive" in the title, it's not necessarily Claircognizant. For instance, seeing a vision of the future (precogitive Clairvoyant), hearing the lotto numbers (precogitive Clairaudient), knowing the elevator will break (Precogitive Claircognitive), feeling someone's oncoming food intolerance (precogitive Clairsentient), smelling the rotting of new milk (precogitive Clairalient), or deciding which ingredients to put in a mixed drink when going to the store even though you've never tasted them for your blind date tonight (precogitive Clairgustant).

Trance: Trance is the ability to enter a different consciousness at the same time as one of your physical senses is released while a psychic one takes over. An example is losing your vision and seeing clearer Clairvoyantly.

Scrying: This is a filter. A psychic connects to the energy of an element, such as water, and uses it to filter and access specific types of information they are seeking. This process is different from gazing, which involves staring. Water scrying, for example, helps to find transient things. So a Clairvoyant will see in his mind, after connecting to the energy signature of the sitter (person being read) and using the energy of water to only find out how his trip to Germany will go for his upcoming vacation.

Why the Zener Card Test Sucked and Why We Need the Archetypes

Karl Zener created the Zener Card Test in the 1930s to test suspected sensitives if they were psychic. J.B. Rhine introduced this at Duke University, but it is an extremely flawed test. You see, potential psychics only needed to get about 25% accuracy in order to call themselves psychics.

I have found, with the story above, that psychics don't always see, and also don't always have details. Let's say Becky is sitting in front of J.B. Rhine. He asks her, "Becky, what do you see on this card?"

Becky says, "I don't know, but I do know you always wanted to be a professional violinist. You were good. You should do that." And she is accurate.

Or Becky says, "I don't know what's on the card, but I do know you have a foot fetish and really want to look under the table at my stockings." And she is accurate. Becky could guess what's on the card, but guessing isn't psychic. It's deductive. Psychics just know. It is certain.

Becky says, "I don't know, but I can see you and Karl over there got into a fight about a sandwich earlier this morning."

Becky can say, "Square," but she is wrong. She then answers "cross," then "circle," then "Butterfly," all of which are wrong. Later, J.B. learns that Becky's list of shapes is identical to the order of shapes that the cards were for the following person (making her precognitive Clairvoyant).

But let's take this further. Let's say that Becky couldn't do that, but could tell Rhine that on his way home, she could see that he will get into an argument with a woman in a blue dress. Or could see that he will be physically sick from the breakfast he had this morning? Or could see how he will have sex with his wife that night but fantasize about one of the participants? All of these are Precognitive Clairvoyant. If Becky could list all of the cards for the following participant because she could see them, Becky is a Precognitive Clairvoyant Lenseborn. If Becky could see the argument, she is a Precognitive Clairvoyant Bondreader. If Becky could see that he will be physically sick from his breakfast food, she is a Precognitive Clairvoyant Physician. If Becky could see his sexual thoughts and encounters, she would be a Precognitive Clairvoyant Harrowbinder. They are all Precognitive. They are all Clairvoyant.

Many psychics can only achieve a few areas. Not everyone can get names of dead relatives (if they are a death medium because they aren't a Veritant) but they can tell you about a specific time that relative did something (an Echoseer). Not everyone can describe a huge event, but they can give you a talent that no one else would know (Luminator). Not all psychics can determine if someone is sick or has an illness, but some can tell you if they have the personality to lie about having an affair (Veritant). It's with these differences that I have broken up the human condition into the Seven Psychic Archetypes.

1s: The Physicians - Overall Wellbeing
2s: The Luminators - Potentials/Hopes
3s: The Harrowbinders - Things Hidden/Shameful
4s: The Echoseers - Events
5s: The Bondreaders - Relationships
6s: The Veritants - Personalities/Essence of
7s: The Lenseborns - Details

1 - The Physician
2 - The Luminators
3 - The Harrowbinders
4 - The Echoseers
5 - The Bondreaders
6 - The Veritants
7 The Lenseborn

Discovery

My OS Clairsentience: A Terrifying Journey

I was terrified when I first discovered I was an Over Sensitive (OS) Clairsentient. The sensations I experienced were overwhelming, at times paralyzing, and far beyond what I had ever anticipated. The most unsettling aspect was when I began to feel physical symptoms that weren't my own.

These were not typical emotional experiences, but stigmata-like manifestations (bruises, cuts, and even swelling on my skin that corresponded to phenomena I could not explain). I would wake up with sensations of pain or discomfort that were not mine, feeling as if my body were a mirror for someone else's suffering. My physical form was reacting to an energetic imprint I had no control over. I felt emotionally flooded with grief, anger, or sorrow that seemed to come from nowhere, leaving me confused and scared. I couldn't understand why I was feeling these intense emotions or physical symptoms, but I knew they weren't originating from my own life.

It wasn't until I was asked to work on a missing person's case and double-check another psychic's work that I began to understand what was happening. I was asked to verify what the other psychic had sensed. To my surprise, as I tuned in, I was experiencing things that I had not been able to do before. I could hear and see things from different angles. I felt things differently and knew different aspects. With this, I explained to those who had elicited my help where the other psychic's mistakes were (misinterpreting, drawing conclusions instead of relaying information, deducing instead of explaining). I learned I could experience exactly what the other psychic had felt, even though I did not possess the same abilities she did. The psychic experiences they had experienced became my own in that moment, and I knew her Claircognizant insights and saw her Clairvoyant visions as though they were mine. I could "step into her shoes" and see the world through her psychic lens, without actually having those abilities myself.

This discovery was both mind-blowing and humbling. I realized that my OS Clairsentience was far more complex than I had initially understood. It wasn't just about feeling other people's emotions or my body reproducing injury from other people; my unique OS could also experience another psychic's abilities as though those Clairs and how they manifested were my own. I had the ability to mirror the perceptions of others by connecting to their energy signature, experiencing their visions, insights, sounds, smells, and impressions as if I were tapping into their Clairabilities directly. This was the moment I began to see the true potential of my gifts, and it ultimately led to a profound shift in how I approached psychic work: Training psychics.

Mirroring the Psychic Experience

As an Over Sensitive (OS) Clairsentient Psychic, my abilities surpass the typical experience of psychic perception. Unlike many psychics who can only access *their* own unique Clairabilities, I have the rare and remarkable capacity to mirror the experiences of others. This this dual-natured ability allows me to fully experience what other psychics are feeling or perceiving, as if their psychic abilities take over my body and I get to watch what they watch or hear what they hear. Through this, I have come to understand the intricacies of my abilities and also the full spectrum of psychic experiences that others have to navigate.

This mirroring phenomenon is incredibly profound, and it's the very reason I began training psychics. Early in my journey, I realized that my Clairsentient abilities weren't just about feeling others' emotions; they also allowed me to feel the exact psychic input of those I connect to. This meant that, when interacting with fellow psychics, I could physically experience their Clairabilities in full, as though I were tapping into their psychic senses and experiencing their gifts firsthand. This ability provided me with a unique and expansive understanding of the psychic world because I could experience ways of working as a psychic that I don't have myself organically.

Experiencing Other Archetypes

One of the most fascinating aspects of my psychic experience is the way my Clairsentient mirroring allowed me to discover and create The Sevens in deeply immersive ways. By mirroring the capabilities of other psychics, I've been able to perceive how the different archetypes operate, not only intellectually but experientially.

For example, as a Clairsentient Psychic, my work is rooted in feeling what happens when I connect to energy, be it the emotions or the physical sensations left behind by people, places, or objects. However, when I "mirror" a Clairvoyant, I find myself experiencing the world through their visionary lens. Suddenly, I perceive what they perceive; images, scenes, and visions unfolding in my mind's eye as vividly as if I were seeing them through their own inner lens. I've felt the dazzling clarity of a Clairvoyant when they see an aura or a specific person's hopes and dreams in vivid detail. This experience is not mine to own, yet I feel as though I am within the image, understanding how that kind of Clairvoyant processes the imagery and builds a psychic narrative from it.

When I connect with a Clairaudient Psychic (which I am not), I suddenly become attuned to the sounds and voices that only they can hear in their head. My experience shifts, and the sounds they perceive, be it a whisper from a conversation they can hear in their head or the thoughts spoken out loud, become so real to me that it's almost as if I'm getting them through my own Clairs. I realize just how much of their emotional depth is tied to their psychic-auditory perception. For the Clairaudient, it's not merely hearing words within; it's feeling the reverberation of those words in their body, understanding the emotional intent behind the sounds.

I've also mirrored Claircognizant Psychics; in those experiences, the sensation of knowing is profound and expansive. With them, I don't see visions or hear sounds. I simply know things that my Claircognizance does not provide. When I mirror their Claircognizance, I suddenly have access to thoughts on relationships, dreams of someone's aspirations, and in a swift, pure understanding that doesn't require logical thought. I feel the immediacy of knowing as though all puzzle pieces have been revealed without effort.

My experiences in my archetypes, such as Harrowbinders and Echoseers, have been equally revealing. As a Harrowbinder, I've experienced the intense emotional energy and sometimes painful clarity someone feels as they dive into repressed memories or shadows. I've felt the way they interact with suppressed fears, trauma, and desires, understanding how they use their abilities to bring hidden truths to light. When I mirror a psychic as a Harrowbinder, I become deeply attuned to the residual emotional energy that the psychic carries with them, just as they do.

Through this mirroring ability, I have learned how the Sevens interact with one another, each offering unique perspectives and strengths. Clairsentients feel the emotional weight of a moment, Clairvoyants visualize it, Clairaudients hear it, and Claircognizants know it; all of these experiences are enriched by the overlapping qualities of the archetypes, leading to a fuller understanding of psychic interaction.

Training Psychics and Discovering the Other Clairs

It was this mirroring ability that led me to begin training psychics. By experiencing their abilities, I learned how different Clairs manifest and interact with one another. As I worked with other psychics, I started to recognize the gaps in my own abilities. For example, while I have a Clairsentient, Clairvoyant, and Claircognizant foundation, I've noticed how some psychics possess abilities I don't naturally experience, like Clairalience or Clairgustance.

My mirroring experiences allowed me to widen my scope of psychic understanding and recognize the distinct layers of perception each Clair brings to the table. When working with psychics who possess precognition or psychokinesis, I could feel the uniqueness of their psychic biology, sometimes sensing future outcomes, other times feeling energetic shifts, or even feeling in my own body how they can tingle in order to make objects move. Through this, I discovered that no single Clair or archetype is complete on its own. The more I experienced the psychic abilities of others, the more I came to understand how the Clairs interconnect.

Through this process, I was able to hone my teaching methods for BearBridge Academy, focusing on helping psychics discover their unique talents and how to expand their perception by learning from each other's strengths. It is through mirroring the experiences of others that I am able to provide a holistic view of psychic development, showing students how they can access their own inherent gifts while also understanding how to broaden their perceptions.

The Evolution of My Psychic Path

My OS Clairsentient mirroring ability has shaped my journey as a psychic. This skill allows me to experience the psychic senses of others, granting me a deeper understanding of the complex, layered world of psychic perception. This ability led me to train psychics, as I could understand the interplay of the Clairs and teach others how to refine their abilities and connect with their gifts.

This mirroring has shown me the vast scope of the psychic world, opening my eyes to dimensions and abilities that would have been difficult to understand through theory alone. It's allowed me to connect with other psychics on a deep level and explore areas of psychic development that I would not have been able to discover on my own.

My work as a teacher and psychic guide is deeply informed by my experiences mirroring others. Mirroring has allowed me to become an authority on psychic abilities and a mentor for psychics, helping them unlock their true potential while deepening my understanding of the infinite range of psychic perception. Through this ability, I continue to explore the expansive nature of psychic work, always discovering new layers and experiences I can share with others.

1s: Physicians

Overall Wellbeing

Just because they access the layer on the outside of the electromagnetic energy, don't assume they are the easiest archetype to identify. The Physician is a psychic tuned to the overall well-being of a person, place, or situation. They sense balance or imbalance in all its forms: physical, emotional, mental, and spiritual. To them, health is not a checklist, but a resonance. A feeling. A shift in the air.

Depending on their Clair gifts, Physicians may read the body through aura, touch, intuition, or energetic impression. They may get a bad feeling about someone and later learn that person was harboring illness, malice, or deep instability. Or they may enter a space and feel peace. What they detect is rarely detailed, but it is true. Subtle doesn't mean shallow. Surface doesn't mean soft. When a Physician says something is "off," it is.

Their gift works like the body itself: mysterious, layered, and alive. These psychics could be healers by nature; many are drawn to that path. Their purpose is to reveal the state of things as they are. They may even have such an impulse to reveal what they know because they want others to do something about it before it's too late.

Physicians can also be given symbols and metaphors instead of exact information which will need interpretation.

1S: PHYSICIANS

The Physician doesn't see what hurts. They know where the pain is trying to hide.
They feel the shift before the storm.

Clairvoyant Physician

(Regular Sensitivity 6–9)

The regular Clairvoyant Physician perceives overall wellness by seeing energy fields and aura colors through their mind's eye. Their Clairvoyant ability gives them broad yet accurate visual insight into the health and energetic state of a person, place, or situation. They may see swirling colors in the aura, each tied to an emotional, mental, physical, or spiritual condition.

They may also find their eyes drawn to specific areas of the body during a reading, sensing that something is "off" in that location. They don't always know the issue, whether it's a bruise or a tumor, but their accuracy in identifying the location of the imbalance is striking.

Clairvoyant Physicians are often mistaken for medical intuitives or spiritual healers. They don't heal, but they reveal.

Many Physicians are called to use their psychic abilities in congruence with a career in healing, feeling they are called. Their role is to detect energetic disturbances and bring them to light before they manifest more deeply or go unnoticed.

Physicians can also have visions of symbols and metaphors instead of exact information regarding situations that the sitter is going through.

CLAIRVOYANT PHYSICIAN

For example:

• A dark green shadow near the chest could signify emotional suppression or grief.

• A sudden pulse of red near the hands may signal inflammation or unexpressed anger.

> *"You don't look sick, but your energy is screaming. Especially right here, around your liver. You might want to check that out."*

OS Clairvoyant Physician

(Over Sensitive – Sensitivity 10)

The Over-Sensitive Clairvoyant Physician experiences psychic sight and physical sight as the same. Their brain cannot distinguish between what is being seen psychically and what is being seen with the physical eyes.

This creates a powerful, but often overwhelming, experience. This can be distressing in public, seeing people appear half-faded, splintered, or shrouded in black mist. Their world is filled with overlaid vision, a synesthetic fusion of energetic data and visual information.

An OS Clairvoyant Physician must learn grounding and separation techniques early in their development, or risk sensory overload, paranoia, or misdiagnosing spiritual impressions as physical reality. A great grounding technique is to feel the floor underneath and then name what their own nervous system feels like.

When trained, however, they become hyper-accurate diagnostic mirrors, seeing what is hidden from both medicine and intuition. They are particularly effective in spaces where conventional diagnostics fall short or when subtle energetic wounds need exposure.

They might:

- See wounds, deformities, or dark marks on people who appear physically healthy
- Perceive colors or shapes clinging to someone's body, indicating energetic trauma
- View phantom symptoms, like seeing someone's face appear bruised when no bruise exists, but an emotional trauma is stored there

> *"Your face keeps shifting. There's this gray film around your jaw. It's not physical, but it's affecting your speech and how people hear you."*

Clairaudient Physician

(Regular Sensitivity 6-9)

The regular Clairaudient Physician receives information about a person's overall well-being through psychic hearing. Rather than using their physical ears, these psychics hear with their minds, receiving sounds, words, tones, or even full songs that correlate to the emotional, physical, mental, or spiritual health of a person or place.

This kind of psychic hears triggers of truth, and their role is to translate what is heard into insight. They don't often hear diagnoses or specific conditions, but rather, energetic clues about areas that need care or further attention.

Clairaudient Physicians are especially attuned to vibrational imbalances. When someone's tone of voice, word choice, or frequency of speech doesn't align with their actual energetic state, they are triggered to hear it in their mind.

CLAIRAUDIENT PHYSICIAN

They often experience:

• Repeating words in their mind when someone mentions a health issue ("back, back, back" when a back injury needs more attention)

• Spontaneous song lyrics or music that relate to a situation (e.g., hearing P!nk's "You Make Me Sick" when someone is describing a toxic relationship or physical illness)

• Pick up medical complaints or emotional expressions from people across the room or across the world

> ***"You keep talking about your migraines, but I just keep hearing the word 'grief' over and over again. I think this may be emotional."***

OS Clairaudient Physician

(Over Sensitive – Sensitivity 10)

The OS Clairaudient Physician experiences no separation between psychic and physical hearing. What they hear feels fully real, as if someone were speaking aloud, even when no physical sound is present. Their psychic perception of energy through sound becomes indistinguishable from reality, sometimes thinking a spirit is talking to them and creating sound waves.

This often leads to misinterpretation by others, as they may appear to be "hallucinating" or experiencing mental health symptoms. In truth, they are picking up the auric echoes of electromagnetic energy and interpreting them through a crossed sensory system.

Their world is filled with auditory cues that don't belong to the physical moment. Unless trained, OS Clairaudients may suffer from:
- Auditory overwhelm
- Paranoia about being "watched" or "whispered to"
- Inability to focus in crowded or emotionally dense environments

Once trained, however, they become extraordinarily precise sound-based diagnostics. They can hear the truth in someone's voice, the pain in a laugh, or the emotional residue of a days-old argument in a room.

They might:
- Tinnitus-like ringing in the ears when something is wrong, either spiritually, energetically, or emotionally
- Hear voices, phrases, or yelling with their physical ears when no one is present
- Perceive trees or buildings crying or whispers from spiritually unwell locations or traumatized spaces

> *"You say you're fine, but I just heard someone scream inside your voice. Like a wail layered underneath. You're not fine."*

Claircognizant Physician

(Regular Sensitivity 6-9)

The regular Claircognizant Physician can "just know" how someone is doing, without being told, taught, or shown. Their insight arises as sudden certainty, often without sensory imagery or emotional charge. It's simply known.

This type of Physician is best thought of as a human wellness radar. They walk into a room or engage with a person and immediately register a state of being: calm, distressed, spiritually blocked, physically drained, energetically fractured, etc.

Unlike other Clairs, they may not perceive the "how" or "why." They just know that something is. They also tend to trust their insight without needing validation, and they're usually right.

Claircognizant Physicians can be given the thoughts of symbols and metaphors instead of exact information regarding situations that the sitter is going through.

CLAIRCOGNIZANT PHYSICIAN

They can detect:
- Emotional suppression
- Underlying spiritual unrest
- Health shifts before physical symptoms emerge

> *"I don't know how I know, but your thyroid feels off. You should have it checked."*
>
> *"You're grieving. You haven't said it, but I know it's there, under the surface."*
>
> *"It's not in your shoulder. It's in your nervous system. I don't know how I know. I just do."*

OS Claircognizant Physician

(Over Sensitive - Sensitivity 10)

The OS Claircognizant Physician operates on an entirely different scale. Their cognitive channels are hyper-attuned, meaning information flows to them constantly, without effort, and often without context.

They don't receive thoughts. They receive truths; entire data sets about someone's state of being that bypass logic or sequence. This kind of mind downloads insight, much like a genius suddenly grasping a theorem they've never studied. They might know that someone's liver is sluggish before the person mentions fatigue.

The OS Claircognizant Physician is often labeled as having intellectual brilliance or invasive perception. In reality, the information is not deduced or observed; it simply exists within their awareness.

When harnessed, however, they become unparalleled insight machines, able to assess well-being at a systemic, spiritual, and emotional level faster than anyone else.

OS CLAIRCOGNIZANT PHYSICIAN

Untamed, they may struggle with:
- Mental fatigue
- Difficulty distinguishing between personal and external insight
- Feeling responsible for others' healing or path

> "You haven't been touched in six months, and your spirit is breaking from it. I don't mean to intrude. I just know."
>
> "You're losing your faith. You won't tell anyone, but I know."

Clairsentient Physician

(Regular Sensitivity 6-9)

The regular Clairsentient Physician receives information about well-being through clear physical and emotional feelings. They don't guess or reason; they feel it in their body or emotions. Often, the area of their body that reacts will mirror the client's imbalance.

Additionally, they may feel a gut instinct about a person or environment.

Clairsentient Physicians are emotionally intuitive, often picking up discomfort, danger, or unrest in others long before it's spoken or visible. They may not always be able to identify the exact cause, but their general sensing is reliably accurate.

They might experience:
- A sudden tightness in their own chest when the sitter has heart issues
- A wave of nausea when sensing emotional or spiritual toxicity
- Goosebumps, shivers, or warmth tied to energy shifts in the room or aura

CLAIRSENTIENT PHYSICIAN

They tend to be described as:
- "Empaths with precision"
- Psychic barometers for energy in people, places, and objects
- Practitioners who feel auras instead of seeing them

> *"I just got a bad feeling when I touched your arm, like a jolt of sadness. Are you okay?"*
>
> *"I don't like this building. There's something wrong in the walls."*

OS Clairsentient Physician

(Over Sensitive - Sensitivity 10)

The OS Clairsentient Physician takes "feeling someone else's experience" to an extreme level. Their nervous system mirrors the energy of the person or place they connect with, often manifesting physical symptoms, intense emotions, or sudden bodily changes that do not originate from themselves.

At this level, their body is not symbolic; it reacts physically to energetic information, often leading to confusion in medical or psychological settings. They may be misdiagnosed with:
- Somatic disorders
- Bipolar symptoms (due to unexplained emotional spikes)
- Psychosomatic illness, or even DID-like body shifts

What's really happening is that their system is mirroring the unspoken or unrecognized experiences of others. When trained, these psychics can provide a deep, experiential diagnosis (human sensors).

With proper training, grounding, and energy management, OS Clairsentients can become the most accurate body-energy translators in the psychic field.

They might:

• Break into a cold sweat and feel chest pressure when standing near someone with a heart condition

• Begin to cry, laugh, or shake with emotion that isn't theirs

• Feel phantom pain, pressure, or sensations in a body part, sometimes even drawing stigmata-like marks on the skin

> *"My hip... it's aching so badly. Oh... no, wait. That's not mine. That's you."*

Clairgustant Physician

(Regular Sensitivity 6-9)

A regular Clairgustant Physician receives psychic information about a person, place, or situation through clear tasting, without ingesting or touching anything. These impressions are usually present as sudden shifts in taste in the mouth, triggered by proximity to or thoughts about a person or space.

These psychics often use taste as a general indicator of well-being.

While they rarely get detailed diagnoses, they are exceptionally skilled at psychically flavoring energy, assigning tastes to unseen truths. This skill is subtle but incredibly effective when paired with discernment and trust in the signal.

CLAIRGUSTANT PHYSICIAN

Examples:
- A sour or metallic taste when entering a room where something is "off"
- A dry mouth sensation when someone is emotionally or spiritually dehydrated
- A sweet aftertaste while in the presence of someone deeply kind or joyous

> *"I get this bitter, stale flavor when I think about your workplace. It doesn't feel like a healthy environment."*
> *"There's this sweetness when you talk about your grandmother. I think she's protecting you spiritually."*

OS Clairgustant Physician

(Over Sensitive – Sensitivity 10)

The OS Clairgustant Physician cannot distinguish between physical taste and psychic taste. Their sensory wiring is cross-firing, so psychic impressions literally manifest in the mouth, as if they have eaten or ingested something, even when they haven't.

This can be disruptive and disorienting, especially in public or emotional settings. Imagine eating dinner and suddenly tasting chemicals or decay, only to realize it's not your food, but someone's trauma seated next to you. It's crucial to ensure a tumor is not present, as it can mimic this psychic sense.

Untrained OS Clairgustants may:
- Suffer from appetite distortion
- Become hyper-sensitive to textures and food environments
- Feel isolated by a sense that others don't believe or understand

But with discipline and filtering techniques, they become extraordinarily energetic tasters, able to discern the presence of emotional/energetic shifts and their flavor, depth, and resonance.

They might:
- Taste blood, bile, rot, or sour milk when interacting with someone sick
- Experience full meals or foreign flavors when tuning in to someone's memory or spirit
- Lose their appetite entirely when overwhelmed by layers of conflicting energetic tastes

> *"There's a coppery taste in my mouth. That usually means fear is lodged in the root chakra. Are you holding something in?"*
> *"This place tastes moldy to me. There's trauma soaked into the walls."*

Clairalient Physician

(Regular Sensitivity 6-9)

The regular Clairalient Physician psychically perceives well-being through smell, often detecting scents that aren't physically present. These smells arise in response to a person's aura, emotional state, health condition, or environment, acting like subtle energetic cues.

Each Clairalient develops a personal scent-language: a unique internal guide that links particular smells with particular psychic impressions.

These psychics don't analyze; they smell and interpret. They can smell if someone is sick or out of alignment. If someone has hidden injuries or infections, they will smell it. An amazing psychic, the Clairalient Physician is like the hounds that can detect cancer with their sense of smell; however, instead of actually smelling, they receive it psychically through the patient's electromagnetic signature.

Clairalient Physicians are incredibly helpful in energetically evaluating spaces and people, especially when those around them may be emotionally guarded or unaware of their own state.

CLAIRALIENT PHYSICIAN

For example:
- The scent of burning wood might signal anger or trauma (often tied to red or black auras)
- A linen-like freshness might reflect peace, spiritual alignment, or healing (often linked to green or blue auras)
- A sudden smell of stale air or mildew might indicate stagnation or blocked emotional energy

> *"I smell lavender and chalk dust. That's my sign, someone's on a spiritual path but also carrying grief."*
>
> *"When you walked in, I got the smell of blood and antiseptic. Have you recently been in a hospital? Or are you supposed to be?"*

OS Clairalient Physician

(Over Sensitive - Sensitivity 10)

The OS Clairalient Physician is unable to separate psychic scent from physical scent. Their olfactory sense is fully intertwined with their psychic perception, and so every energetic impression is received as a literal smell.

In public, this can be a nightmare: they might recoil at invisible stenches, lose focus due to a sudden whiff of burning rubber, or be unable to eat when a nearby table carries the scent of spiritual toxicity.

Untrained, they are prone to:
- Headaches, nausea, or dizziness due to scent overload
- Emotional exhaustion from involuntary reactions
- Deep confusion when no one else can confirm what they "smell"

But when refined and controlled, OS Clairalient Physicians are extraordinarily sensitive energy translators, capable of detecting layered nuances in a person's field or a room's atmosphere that would go unnoticed by any other Clair.

They might:

• Smell decay or rot when someone is spiritually sick or harboring repressed rage

• Catch the scent of perfume, smoke, or flowers linked to passed loved ones or emotional memory

• Experience olfactory overload in environments with dense or conflicting energy signatures

> *"I smell charred cinnamon. That's what I get when someone is carrying rage dressed up as charm."*
>
> *"I know it's not really there, but it smells like your grandmother's kitchen. I think she's nearby, spiritually."*

2s: Luminators

Hopes, Dreams, and Potentials

They do not search for shadows; they know the light. The Luminator perceives the hopes, dreams, aspirations, and untapped potential that hum beneath the surface of a person's being. Where others see uncertainty, they see radiance. To a Luminator, the possible shines brighter than the present.

Their gift is focused entirely on what could be; the best version of a person, a moment, or a path. They look into a crowd and know, without question, who would thrive as a leader, a healer, an artist. Even if the person doesn't yet believe it. Even if they've never shown it. Luminators are drawn to potential like light to mirrors, and in this way, they reflect the highest possible outcomes back to others. Their presence can feel like luck, like gravity shifting in your favor. They are your personal luck dragon.

But their clarity is not destiny. And that is their curse. The Luminator may offer insight so vivid, so specific, that it sounds like a prediction, but it is not the future. It is the best possible outcome for it, not a guarantee. They may give the numbers to a lottery, only to be told they were wrong, not because they lied, but because the numbers reflected the highest winning possibility, not the actual event. The Luminator sees what could shine brightest, not what will. And for that reason, they are often mistaken for Lenseborns or precognitive psychics.

2S: LUMINATORS

Rarest among readers, Luminators are a quiet force in the world. Their ability to access the electromagnetic frequency of positive potential is powerful, but it is subtle, and often overlooked. In a world wired for fear and survival, few sit with genuine curiosity about another person's dreams. Fewer still believe in them.

> ***The Luminator does not tell you who you are. They tell you who you could be... if you dared.***
> ***They don't light the way. They show you where you already shine.***

Clairvoyant Luminator

(Regular Sensitivity 6-9)

The regular Clairvoyant Luminator sees what shines within someone as a vision. Not who they are, but who they could become. When they connect with a sitter, they receive visual flashes of that person's deepest hopes, unrealized dreams, hidden desires, and untapped potential.

These visions are not predictive; they are invitational. The Luminator sees only the best-case potential, the shining version of the self that could come forward with nurturing and belief. They do not see failure, danger, or destiny, only possibility rooted in desire.

Because their visions are so vivid and specific, Clairvoyant Luminators are often mistaken for precognitive seers. But they are not predicting what will happen; they are revealing what could happen if the sitter follows the pull of their own longing.

They are excellent for helping clients make decisions based on destiny alignment, not fear, and often act as mirrors of inner light, reminding people of what they once dared to want.

They might see:

- A violin, representing a long-abandoned dream of becoming a musician
- A stage, a book, a canvas, or sunlight pouring into a garden: the symbolic expressions of the sitter's brightest possible path
- A vision of the sitter in their ideal future, often emotionally elevated and symbolically rich

> *"I see you painting on a large white wall. There's so much light. It feels like freedom. Have you ever dreamed of being an artist?"*

OS Clairvoyant Luminator
(Over Sensitive - Sensitivity 10)

The OS Clairvoyant Luminator does not just see visions of someone's potential. They become immersed in the sitter's potential through visions. The line between the sitter's deepest desires and the Luminator's own visual experience becomes blurred, making it difficult to distinguish between imagination and psychic truth. They may also mistake the desires, hobbies, and skills of others as their own new interests.

These visions can be so detailed and sensory-rich that they may begin to interpret them as real futures, leading to frustration when their "prediction" doesn't come true. The OS Luminator may feel emotionally destabilized when others do not pursue the dream they've seen so clearly.

Untrained, they might:
- Give overly specific predictions (mistaking potential for certainty)
- Attach emotionally to the sitter's vision or outcome
- Experience sensory echo (feeling like they played the violin, sang the song, or lived the life)

Trained, however, they become living reflections of divine potential, offering detailed, inspiring images that revive the dreams long buried. They are not fortune-tellers. They are light-bringers.

They might:

• See an entire daydream unfold like a movie, feeling emotionally swept into the narrative

• Lose track of where the sitter's dream ends and their personal hopes begin

• Experience overwhelm or longing from someone else's unlived life

> *"You're standing on a balcony with the wind in your hair, holding a novel you wrote. The cover is orange, and your name is embossed in gold. I don't know if you'll publish it, but I know you could. That's what your soul wants."*

Clairaudient Luminator

(Regular Sensitivity 6-9)

The regular Clairaudient Luminator perceives the hopes, dreams, and potential of others through psychic sound. They may hear words, music, phrases, mantras, or affirmations that reflect a person's deepest inner aspirations, even those that the sitter has forgotten or dismissed.

This Clair gives voice to the soul's longing. Clairaudient Luminators hear not what has happened, but what wants to be. The tones, melodies, and words they receive point toward the sitter's highest vibrational alignment, often with emotional resonance.

They are gentle messengers, like receiving a song from the future self, or an echo from a dream not yet born. And they are often most helpful to clients who are at a crossroads and need to remember what they truly long for.

They might hear:
- A childhood song tied to a long-lost creative dream
- The word "teacher" whispered softly, even if the sitter never considered that path
- A refrain like "you were meant for more" echoing over and over in their mind

> *"I keep hearing the phrase, 'She leads with her heart.' I think you're meant to be in a role where your compassion is your strength."*

OS Clairaudient Luminator

(Over Sensitive - Sensitivity 10)

The OS Clairaudient Luminator is deeply immersed in the sound of someone's soul, often to the point of confusion between psychic input and physical sound. Their mind receives audio-like downloads so vivid that it feels like someone is speaking aloud, or like music is being played just outside the room.

These psychics are especially sensitive to the emotional vibration of the words or sounds they hear. A single whispered word can move them to tears if it reflects a dream buried under years of shame or disappointment.

Untrained OS Clairaudients may:
- Misattribute psychic sound as their own inner voice or "spirit guide"
- Become overwhelmed in crowded places where energetic noise is too loud
- Struggle with insomnia or dissociation due to constant subconscious input

When trained and grounded, however, they are able to give voice to the unspoken potential in others, expressing, often with uncanny phrasing, the exact desire the sitter didn't know they were waiting to hear.

They may:

- Hear entire songs or speeches someone has never voiced aloud, but deeply desires to express
- Mistake psychic audio for literal sound (e.g., turning around because they "heard" someone say "I want to dance again")
- Become emotionally swept into lyrics or lines that carry the sitter's dormant longing

> *"You may not say it, but I heard you humming a lullaby in your soul. I think you want to be a mother. Or a nurturer, in some way."*
>
> *"I keep hearing you singing. And I don't think it's metaphorical."*

Claircognizant Luminator

(Regular Sensitivity 6-9)

The regular Claircognizant Luminator possesses a powerful form of "clear knowing" that is focused not on current states or past events, but on a person's potential and purpose.

Their gift is rooted in certainty, not observation, logic, or guesswork. When they connect to someone, they simply know what that person is meant for.

They do not see detailed visions or hear poetic phrases. Instead, they grasp potential as a truth, a flash of inner clarity about what aligns most powerfully with the sitter's soul. Their insights are often sudden, striking, and deeply affirming.

They are especially helpful to people who have multiple paths or gifts and don't know which one is the right fit.

CLAIRCOGNIZANT LUMINATOR

Claircognizant Luminators are excellent at:
- Identifying the best environment or career for someone's personal fulfillment
- Recognizing the core truth beneath self-doubt or confusion
- Suggesting next steps not based on reason, but on resonance

> *"You're meant to lead. I don't know why I know this, but you won't be fulfilled until you do."*
> *"You should be writing. That's where your light lives."*
> *"You light up when you teach. You may not see yourself as a teacher, but your energy says otherwise."*

OS Claircognizant Luminator

(Over Sensitive - Sensitivity 10)

The OS Claircognizant Luminator doesn't just know a person's potential, they embody it for a moment. Their mind becomes flooded with downloads of purpose, to the point that it can feel as though they are living the sitter's possible future. The insight arrives without process or pause, pure clarity, often overwhelming in its intensity.

This kind of psychic bypasses the need for symbols, images, or metaphors. They receive pure understanding, a kind of psychic blueprint of who someone is capable of becoming. But because the knowing is so complete, it can be hard for them to:
• Avoid becoming emotionally attached to outcomes
• Distinguish their own ambitions from what they're receiving from others

Untamed, they may come across as pushy or overly confident in skills for which they have not practiced. But when trained, OS Claircognizant Luminators are brilliant activators of destiny, pointing others toward alignment with unwavering clarity.

They may:

• Know someone's ideal profession, lifestyle, or destiny within seconds of meeting them

• Know the jargon, information, or even be able to test like an expert in the same area the sitter can without being taught the information

> *"You are supposed to speak. That is your gift. If you're not using your voice, you're betraying your own potential."*

Clairsentient Luminator

(Regular Sensitivity 6-9)

The regular Clairsentient Luminator feels a person's potential in their body and emotional system. Rather than seeing visions or hearing messages, they experience intuitive emotion or physical sensation in response to someone's dreams, hopes, and aligned path.

They may not be able to articulate it right away. This type of Luminator is a soul barometer. They feel what the sitter's highest reality feels when a path or possibility is named. Their gift is one of confirmation through sensation.

They are especially helpful for:
- People who don't know what they want, but react emotionally when the truth is named
- Sitters struggling with choice because the Clairsentient Luminator can physically feel which option aligns most fully
- Encouraging the felt sense of hope to resurface in someone who has suppressed it

They might:

- Feel a surge of joy when someone talks about a dream they've never pursued
- Experience a warm, full-body glow when someone says something that aligns with their true calling
- Get goosebumps or an inner lift when a sitter is on the verge of discovering their next best step

> *"Whatever you just said... yes. That felt right. My chest opened up when you mentioned traveling."*
>
> *"When you talked about working with animals, my stomach calmed completely. That tells me something."*

OS Clairsentient Luminator

(Over Sensitive - Sensitivity 10)

The OS Clairsentient Luminator doesn't just feel someone's potential; they embody it. Their nervous system reacts so strongly to the sitter's dream state or aspirational energy that they may mistake those longings as their own, or even experience emotional overwhelm from the intensity of unrealized potential.

Because they feel others' dreams as deep emotional resonance, OS Clairsentient Luminators can:
- Become physically or emotionally affected by sitters who deny or sabotage their own goals
- Struggle with emotional boundaries, especially when others have large or untapped potential
- Be mistaken for moody, overly empathic, or emotionally unstable if not trained

However, when grounded and channeled, they are some of the most motivational and healing psychic guides in the archetype system. They remind the sitter what it feels like to hope again. Not in words, but in the body.

They may:
- Burst into tears when someone talks about a buried dream
- Feel euphoric, dizzy, or overcome with joy when in the presence of someone stepping into alignment
- Sense visceral frustration, pressure, or nausea when someone speaks against their own aspirations

> *"When you said 'chef,' I felt it in my whole body... like light spread through my arms. I think that's the dream. And I think it's still alive. I can feel the euphoria of cooking."*

Clairgustant Luminator

(Regular Sensitivity 6-9)

The regular Clairgustant Luminator receives intuitive information about a person's hopes, dreams, and potential through the psychic sense of taste. These impressions don't involve physical food or drink. They arrive as spontaneous flavor sensations in the mouth, triggered by a person's energy field or when speaking about certain possibilities.

Examples:
- A burst of sweetness when someone talks about a long-held but abandoned dream
- A bright citrus zing when a new opportunity is in alignment
- A cool, fresh flavor (like mint or cucumber) when someone names a possibility that would bring them peace and freedom

These psychics use taste as a metaphor, the energetic flavor of a dream or destiny point shows up as a real-time tasting experience. They don't always know the meaning immediately, but they'll interpret based on their intuitive palate.

CLAIRGUSTANT LUMINATOR

Clairgustant Luminators are especially good at:

- Validating a client's true longing or path based on how it tastes energetically
- Offering subtle confirmation or redirection using sensory language
- Helping someone emotionally connect to their own dreams through sensory intuition

> *"When you mentioned studying abroad, my mouth filled with this honeyed taste... like joy that's been waiting a long time."*
> *"There's a bitterness when you talk about staying in your current job. That doesn't feel like your path."*

Os Clairgustant Luminator

(Over Sensitive - Sensitivity 10)

The OS Clairgustant Luminator experiences no separation between psychic taste and physical sensation. When tuning into someone's potential or future path, they don't just taste a flavor metaphorically, they literally experience it in their mouth, as if they've just eaten it.

Because the input is somatic and overwhelming, these psychics can:
- Lose their appetite during emotionally intense sessions
- Crave or avoid certain foods that mirror a client's path or energy
- Struggle with overstimulation or confusion when too many people's dreams are present at once

Untrained, they may:
- Feel emotionally hijacked by the sensory data
- Struggle to explain their impressions to sitters unfamiliar with psychic taste
- Dismiss their own experiences as "weird" or embarrassing

But when refined, OS Clairgustant Luminators become powerful taste trackers of destiny, able to describe the texture, sweetness, sharpness, or emptiness of a path with remarkable clarity.

They may:
- Taste sweet wine or fruit when someone speaks about their dream life
- Experience a flood of cloying sugar or artificial sweetness when someone is chasing an inauthentic fantasy
- Have a dry, metallic, or chalky taste when a person suppresses their potential

> *"You keep saying you don't want to teach, but every time you talk about it, my mouth fills with this fresh vanilla cream flavor. That's what I get when someone is hiding their joy."*

Clairalient Luminator

(Regular Sensitivy 6-9)

The regular Clairalient Luminator receives psychic information about a person's aspirations, dreams, and potential through scent impressions that are not physically present. These scents arise intuitively when the Luminator tunes into a person's energetic field or when a possibility is spoken that aligns (or misaligns) with the sitter's soul.

They might smell:
- Fresh-cut grass or blooming flowers when someone's dream is rooted in growth and peace
- Baking bread or warm vanilla when a potential is tied to nurturing, comfort, or creative fulfillment
- Ozone or rain when a sitter is standing on the edge of a major shift into alignment

Each Clairalient Luminator develops their own internal scent-symbolism, a personal dictionary of aromas that represent the energetic "scent" of a dream.

CLAIRALIENT LUMINATOR

They excel at:

- Helping sitters emotionally connect to their purpose through sensory metaphor
- Sensing when someone is lying to themselves about their goals
- Describing a potential path in vivid, scent-rich emotional language

> *"When you mentioned going back to school, I got the smell of pencils and paper and rain. It feels like home, doesn't it?"*
> *"That business plan smells like stale coffee to me. It's more of an obligation than aspiration."*

OS Clairalient Luminator

(Over Sensitive - Sensitivity 10)

The OS Clairalient Luminator experiences psychic smells as intensely real, immediate, and physically present, even when no source is nearby. Their olfactory system doesn't just translate energy into scent; it immerses them in it.

This can be emotionally powerful but also overwhelming. OS Clairalient Luminators may recoil at the scent of inauthentic aspirations. They might also smell things hours before the sitter speaks a truth. Sometimes they can become emotionally flooded by nostalgic or emotionally charged aromas tied to others' longings.

Untrained, they may:
- Think something in the environment is "off" when it's actually psychic
- Lose trust in their own perception
- Become physically sensitive to strong smells due to the overlap in sensory pathways

Trained and grounded, though, OS Clairalient Luminators are exquisitely attuned to the scent of soul potential. They know when something smells like longing or when a dream is perfumed with fear or fantasy instead of truth.

They might:

• Smell the ocean when someone dreams of freedom, even if they're in a landlocked building

• Be hit with a wave of cologne, sugar, or smoke when someone speaks about a path they desire but won't admit to

• Have a word trigger a sense that is specific to the sitter (a synesthetic response)

> ***"When you talked about opening that café, I smelled cardamom and orange peel. That's what I smell when someone's dream is real and sweet and alive."***

3s: Harrowbinders

The Hidden & The Darkness

They sit in shadows: the hidden, the muck, the ugly, the shameful, the lustful... They are the investigator, finding the aspects that are concealed away. The Harrowbinder is a psychic who draws forth what has been buried: shame, lies, fear, suppressed desires, and the pieces of the human experience that most try to forget. They do not judge what they find because they learn that all areas have ugly sides, hidden or repressed fantasies, making all people an even playing field. Their gift is neutral, revealing what is hidden, in everyone. And we all have something hidden.

Harrowbinders can uncover the truth beneath the performance. They may see the memory no one wants to admit, the craving no one speaks aloud, or the secret someone has told no one, not even out loud to themselves. This includes sexual desires, violent thoughts, fantasies of power or submission, and the unspoken potential to destroy, deceive, or consume. These are not predictions, nor personality traits; they are psychic revelations of what lives in the psyche, not whether the sitter will act on them. For instance, we've all had a raging fantasy. The Harrowbinder will know yours and everyone else's. This work is not evil. It is human. The Harrowbinder offers a mirror for us to reflect our darkness. Their clarity is not rooted in judgment but in accuracy. They see what was hidden, what was denied, and what now asks to be seen.

3S: HARROWBINDERS

> *The Harrowbinder does not tell you who you could be. They show you the part of yourself you hoped no one would ever name.*
> *You don't need to be forgiven to be seen. You just need to stop lying to yourself.*

Clairvoyant Harrowbinder

(Regular Sensitivity 6-9)

The regular Clairvoyant Harrowbinder receives literal psychic visions of what others have buried: shame, trauma, deceit, unspoken desires, and painful memories. Their gift is not a metaphor or dreamscape. The visions are a clear window into the suppressed truth. They see what was, what is still held inside, and what has been hidden in darkness.

These psychics do not interpret symbols or archetypes. They observe reality as it exists within the psychic field. The scenes may be emotionally difficult, but they are specific, detailed, and literal. Clairvoyant Harrowbinders are shown the things most people try to forget, deny, or cover, and they are unflinching in their ability to look.

Their role is not to condemn but to reveal. They bring light to what has been exiled within the self. Think of them as a private investigator.

Clairvoyant Harrowbinders help sitters:
- Help with missing persons
- Uncover the true source of shame or pain
- Find the truth when others are lying or deceiving the sitter

They may witness:
- An ashamed sitter being yelled at by their father as a child
- A sex act connected to power, control, kink, or secrecy
- A moment of manipulation, theft, or betrayal, seen exactly as it happened or was fantasized

> *"He is standing at the kitchen sink, washing blood off a knife. It's not a metaphor. It's something that has happened... something you're trying not to know."*
>
> *"I see you in your ex's bedroom. You're not speaking. You feel like you owe him something. That moment hasn't left your body."*

OS Clairvoyant Harrowbinder

(Over Sensitive - Sensitivity 10)

The OS Clairvoyant Harrowbinder doesn't just see the shadow, they enter it. Their gift is a total psychic immersion into the literal, unfiltered truth of what the sitter has hidden. Their visions are so vivid and exact that they feel as if they are witnessing memory in real-time, complete with sensory detail, emotional charge, and behavioral nuance.

If the sitter lies, omits, or even unconsciously distorts a memory, the vision halts or glitches. The OS Clairvoyant Harrowbinder sees the narrative stop, like a film that's been edited mid-reel. They are uniquely attuned to the presence of fabrication, not because they analyze, but because the psychic feed itself refuses to continue when untruth is introduced. These psychics are not seeing possibilities, dreams, or metaphors. They are watching raw, uncut psychic playback, truth that has been pushed to the farthest corners of the psyche.

Untrained, they may:
- Become emotionally overwhelmed or physically reactive
- Confuse their own emotions with the intensity of what they are witnessing
- Feel haunted by the visions if they are not grounded or spiritually protected

OS CLAIRVOYANT HARROWBINDER

Trained, however, OS Clairvoyant Harrowbinders are among the most fearless and necessary guides in the psychic world. They do what no one else is willing to do: look directly at the truth, the full, undressed, unvarnished human condition, and offer it back without judgment.

They may see:

• A memory of being sexually touched during childhood, even if the sitter has repressed or rationalized it

• A past moment of violence or cruelty for a situation they have been given to look into or to find who has fantasized about extorting their employer

• A scene of humiliation, rage, or obsession, experienced in full literal detail

> *"You said the assault happened in the living room. But I'm seeing a bathroom. That's where it really happened, isn't it?"*
> *"You're telling me you loved him. But in the vision, you're looking at him with disgust. Which one is true?"*

Clairaudient Harrowbinder

(Regular Sensitivity 6-9)

The regular Clairaudient Harrowbinder hears the unspoken truths of the subconscious and hidden: the repressed thoughts, traumatic echoes, and private inner dialogues a person hides even from themselves. This is not symbolic or metaphorical; what they hear is literal psychic audio, often in the voice of the sitter or of someone tied to the original wound or experience.

These psychics can hear both past and present thoughts as long as they are connected to themes of shame, desire, trauma, guilt, or deceit. Sometimes the words are still active in the sitter's psyche, playing beneath their awareness. Other times, they are old echoes lodged deep within the memory field.

Their role is to name what was silenced, not with judgment, but with clarity. They are able to hold space for darkness without reacting to it, becoming invaluable allies for those ready to confront what they've buried.

CLAIRAUDIENT HARROWBINDER

They may hear:
- The exact words a father screamed during a childhood punishment
- A partner's insult that still loops inside the sitter's nervous system
- A whispered internal thought like "You're disgusting," or "I wanted it to hurt."

> *"You say you're fine, but I keep hearing, 'It's my fault. I ruined it.' That thought is still alive in you."*

OS Clairaudient Harrowbinder
(Over Sensitive - Sensitivity 10)

The OS Clairaudient Harrowbinder is fully immersed in the auditory dimension of shadow. They hear the psychic voices, and those voices live inside them. Their system receives shadow-based psychic audio as if it were physical sound, often with no distinction between what is internal and what is external.

Without training, this level of sensitivity can be disorienting and terrifying. But when supported, the OS Clairaudient Harrowbinder becomes one of the clearest channelers of repressed psychic truth, able to hear the thoughts that people are too ashamed to speak or too wounded to remember.

This confusion may manifest as:
- Belief that they are "hearing demons" because the topics are taboo
- Thinking intrusive thoughts are their own
- Feeling haunted by voices that vanish when they leave a specific person or space

In this sensitivity range, they may also misattribute psychic voices to themselves, especially if the content is disturbing. This often leads OS Clairaudients to believe they are being attacked by spirit obsession or haunted, when in fact they are tapping into the shadows of someone near them.

They may hear:
• Present-moment thoughts of others nearby that are laced with fear, self-loathing, or suppressed urges
• Repetitive inner dialogue like "She'll leave you just like the others" or "I hate fucking wetbacks"
• Words spoken years ago that are still energetically active: "Don't tell anyone or I'll kill you"

> *"When you tell the story, I hear your tone stay steady. But within your story, someone is screaming, 'Stop touching me.'"*
> *"I think these voices are mine or some demon, but they're not. I'm sitting next to someone who's never admitted what they want to do..."*

CLAIRCOGNIZANT HARROWBINDER

(REGULAR SENSITIVITY 6-9)

The regular Claircognizant Harrowbinder just knows, not through visions or voices, but through instant, unshakable truth. Their gift uncovers the core of hidden thoughts, including shame-based emotions, deep fear, trauma, and repressed sexual fantasies. They know what others keep from themselves.

Because of this, Claircognizant Harrowbinders may become psychic seducers, not manipulators, but mirrors. They intuit what someone wants sexually and relationally, not as guesswork, but as knowing. This makes them powerful in intimacy because they can offer connection without the danger of rejection. What they give is precisely what the other secretly craves.

They can offer healing with emotional and erotic gratification by naming, witnessing, and sometimes responding to desires that others are afraid to reveal. They also know when someone is lying or trying to hide something.

This includes:
- The unspoken desire to dominate, submit, destroy, or be destroyed
- Guilt from a decision that was never publicly acknowledged
- Emotional patterns driven by longing, fear, or self-betrayal

> *"Lay down. You don't have to have control. I'll take it from here."*
>
> *"That was a lie. You're not scared of being left. You're scared of being seen."*

OS Claircognizant Harrowbinder

(Over Sensitive - Sensitivity 10)

The OS Claircognizant Harrowbinder downloads entire truths in a single breath, sexual, psychological, emotional, and historical. They don't simply understand someone's shadow; they become aware of it as a complete psychic file, with no filter between themselves and the sitter's most private internal world.

They are empathic, accurate responses to desire, acted on only if ethically and emotionally aligned.

Untrained, however, they may:
- Confuse their own needs with those they're reading
- Take on others' shadows as their own
- Have secondary trauma from living memories from people's repressed corners

Trained, they are unparalleled at navigating the erotic and emotional underworld, able to name, reflect, and even fulfill desires that have never been spoken aloud.

They know:
- Sexual fantasies and cravings, including those the person has never admitted
- Hidden prejudices and hatreds, even if the sitter doesn't act on them
- Being a human lie detector

> "You want to be a priest, but you're afraid you won't have a sex life while being a man of the cloth."
>
> "I know a man named James is texting you and that you're cheating on me. He is texting you right now. Look at your phone."

Clairsentient Harrowbinder

(Regular Sensitivity 6-9)

The regular Clairsentient Harrowbinder senses emotion from the residue of unspoken trauma, forbidden desire, and internalized shame. Their nervous system acts as a psychic mirror, pulling in the emotional echo of whatever the sitter has buried.

Clairsentient Harrowbinders feel what others won't admit, not to dramatize, but to name what's real. They are emotional archivists of the human shadow.

These psychics do not guess how someone feels. They become it, momentarily inhabiting the hidden feeling the sitter won't acknowledge. The emotions are real, embodied, and often taboo:

- Sexual disgust
- Violent pleasure
- Jealousy laced with longing
- Emotional numbness from repeated moral failure

CLAIRSENTIENT HARROWBINDER

They may:
• Suddenly feel waves of humiliation from an affair that someone had that ended in secrecy
• Mirror the rage of a child who fantasized about killing their abuser
• Be filled with deep self-loathing, triggered not by the sitter's words, but by their silence

> *"You don't just feel sad to me. You're ashamed that it still turns you on."*
> *"You're pretending to be over it. But inside, you're still begging him to come back and hurt you."*

OS Clairsentient Harrowbinder
(Over Sensitive - Sensitivity 10)

The OS Clairsentient Harrowbinder doesn't stop at the feeling. They physically manifest the psychic injuries they read, mirroring pain, trauma, and buried memories with stigmatic accuracy. Their body becomes the canvas of the shadow.

These are not metaphors. The OS Harrowbinder's nervous system replicates the bodily truth that was never spoken or validated. When someone says, "It wasn't that bad," the Harrowbinder's body will expose the lie, not by accusation, but by embodiment.

Untrained, these psychics are often misdiagnosed with chronic illness, psychosomatic disorders, or dissociation, but what's happening is raw psychic mirroring, a sacred witnessing of what someone else has suffered or silenced.

They also experience:
- Emotional possession, sudden eruptions of rage, lust, dread, grief, or numbness that are not their own
- Panic attacks or fainting triggered by energetic or repressed trauma
- Bleeding from hidden events without wounds or cuts

OS CLAIRSENTIENT HARROWBINDER

Trained, OS Clairsentient Harrowbinders are living testimony to the impact of what goes unspoken. They offer sitters an opportunity not just to feel, but to finally see their own pain reflected with accuracy, courage, and zero shame.

They may:

• Break out in bruising, swelling, or scratches that align with a sitter's past abuse

• Feel constriction in the throat during a session where sexual silencing or coercion occurred

• Show the same symptoms of someone else's heart attack while they are having a heart attack but without the causation

> *"You're saying you were never hit, but my ribs are bruising as we talk."*
>
> *"You told me you don't regret it. Then why do I feel like vomiting when you mention his name?"*

Clairgustant Harrowbinder

(Regular Sensitivity 6-9)

The regular Clairgustant Harrowbinder receives psychic truth through literal taste, with a palate trained on darkness. They don't taste memories, they taste lies, buried guilt, secret perversions, emotional rot, and relational decay. Their mouth reacts like an exposed nerve when something doesn't match what's being spoken.

Clairgustant Harrowbinders are incredibly sensitive to deception and repression. Their psychic taste buds aren't just picking up the truth; they're testing for contamination. And they never swallow what doesn't sit right.

They are also able to detect energetically poisoned or tampered food, whether spiritual, emotional, or literal. Sexual fantasies or power dynamics as distinct flavor profiles, especially when unacknowledged are other manifestations for the Cliargustant Harrowbinder.

They might experience:
- A bitter chemical taste when a client lies, especially about their own intentions
- The flavor of spoiled milk, copper, or bile when speaking about repressed abuse or internalized shame
- A sudden, sugary sweetness that sours into mold or metal when someone is masking desire with moral restraint

> *"When you talk about him, my tongue goes numb. That's how I know you're hiding something."*
> *"This story tastes like plastic... manufactured, rehearsed... You're leaving something out."*

OS Clairgustant Harrowbinder

(Over Sensitive - Sensitivity 10)

The OS Clairgustant Harrowbinder is a walking shadow-taster, whose body reacts with full sensory intensity to anything hidden, rotten, or false. Their tongue becomes a psychic filter, detecting emotional poison, sexual distortion, shame-laced memory, and relational deception with painful clarity.

The response is physical. These psychics may suddenly spit, lose their appetite, start choking, or experience intense cravings or aversions, often tied to what the sitter cannot say.

They can also detect violations of bodily autonomy:
• Tasting bitterness when someone pretends a sexual encounter was consensual
• Feeling a burning sourness when a victim takes the blame for what someone else did
• Being flooded with the taste of soap, pennies, or rot when listening to someone protect an abuser

OS CLAIRGUSTANT HARROWBINDER

Untrained OS Clairgustants may suffer from eating disorders, sensory processing issues, or psychosomatic nausea. But what's really happening is psychic ingestion of the unspoken.

Trained, the OS Clairgustant Harrowbinder becomes a dark sommelier of truth, tasting shadow like its wine, and describing it without flinching. They name what others can't stomach.

They may:

• Gag or vomit when someone lies outright, especially when the lie is about safety, consent, or violence

• Taste blood, semen, bile, or spoiled food during discussions involving repressed sexual trauma or internalized guilt

• React to spiritual poisoning, tasting rancid metal or mold when food, wine, or offerings have been spiritually or energetically corrupted

> *"You're saying you enjoyed it. But it tastes like burnt sugar and vinegar when you speak. That's how I know you're lying."*
> *"This food wasn't just prepared badly, it's energetically tainted. Someone cooked this while hating you."*

Clairalient Harrowbinder
(Regular Sensitivity 6-9)

The regular Clairalient Harrowbinder receives literal psychic scent impressions tied to repressed trauma, hidden guilt, sexual secrets, lies, and emotional decay. The smells are not symbolic; they are triggered responses to real, psychic repression, denial, or hiding embedded in the sitter's energy or the space they occupy.

These psychics are the truth, metabolized through the Harrowbinder's psychic nose.

They are particularly useful in:
- Energetically clearing spaces by identifying lingering shame or trauma
- Pinpointing emotional dynamics that have "gone sour" in relationships
- Naming the presence of ongoing denial, addiction, or self-sabotage

They may smell:
- Rotting meat or mildew when someone is hiding the truth about violence or abuse
- Old cologne, cigarettes, or body odor tied to a past lover who still haunts the psyche
- Bleach, blood, or rust during conversations involving repressed sexual shame or bodily violation

> *"You're telling me you don't want her, but I smell latex and cheap soap. You're not being honest."*
> *"There's something exciting in your energy. I smell opium. Do you want to... go upstairs, sexy?"*

OS Clairalient Harrowbinder

(Over Sensitive - Sensitivity 10)

The OS Clairalient Harrowbinder physically smells the truth of what others try to conceal. Their system doesn't filter scent impressions as psychic but instead projects them directly into their sensory experience, often in overwhelming and disorienting ways.

This can happen in real-time and is not subtle. They may need to leave a space, gag, or begin physically reacting, not to anything present, but to what the energy holds.

Untrained, these psychics may suffer from migraines, phantom smell disorders, or anxiety. But in truth, their body is alchemizing spiritual refuse into something smellable.

Trained, the OS Clairalient Harrowbinder becomes a living scent archive of psychic truth, tracking all things hidden.

They may:
• Smell rotting flesh or burning hair when standing near someone who has committed or endured violence
• Catch the scent of urine, semen, blood, bleach, or vomit when someone is lying about sexual trauma or physical shame
• Experience overpowering smells of alcohol, sweat, or decomposition in spaces where addiction, abuse, or death have gone unspoken

OS Clairalients also:

- Smell spiritual or emotional contamination in food, objects, or offerings
- React violently to false narratives, smelling cloying perfume, rotting fruit, or burning wires when someone lies to their face
- Smell scents of euphoria linked to others' guilt, fetishism, fantasy, or abuse

> *"When you walked in, I smelled dirty sheets and burnt hair. That's not a metaphor. Something happened in your past that you haven't named."*
>
> *"I know where the body is. She was kidnapped near ocean water and I smell sawdust and chocolate. I think she was raped."*

4s: E*choseers*

Events

Where others see static, they sense the story. The Echoseer simply watches footage or glances at a photo. Sometimes a space can capture more than an image. Sometimes someone's words carry more than their voice. The Echoseer listens with senses tuned beyond the visible and gets the bigger picture.

Most of the time, they experience a wide, unfocused sight. They perceive panoramas, the emotional weather of a moment, and the length and weight of memory spread out over time. In doing so, they often miss the close-up, the personal, the intimate detail (unless they are also a 7). Faces blur. Words slip. Their gift is breadth, not precision.

They are best with the unseen tension between people, the silence in a hallway, and the unseen movement before an action. They reveal what shaped the moment, not always what happened within it. In other words, they perceive broader pictures or movies. Echoseers are those who watch/know/hear scenes. This is what is commonly portrayed in movies, television, and other popular depictions of psychics.

4S: ECHOSEERS

> *The Echoseer does not zoom in. They open wide, and see what lingers in the space between seconds.*
> *Clarity is for others. Theirs is the gift of the echo.*

Clairvoyant Echoseer

(Regular Sensitivity 6-9)

The regular Clairvoyant Echoseer receives literal visual echoes of events, emotions, and energy imprints as images, photos, or video footage. They do not see the future (unless they are also precognitive), nor do they witness detail-level reality. What they see is broad, sweeping, environmental, and emotionally charged, like a psychic drone camera hovering over the memory field of the moment.

Their visions are literal, but not magnified. They cannot read fine text on a document in a vision, identify someone's necklace, or tell you what's behind a closed drawer. Their gift is field perception, not detail mining.

Echoseers are especially valuable when reviewing crime scene photos, missing person cases, or surveillance footage and listening to stories. They will have visions of what has happened, and because they see big picture, they may be able to notice details in the background like weather, time of day, or season, all because they have a broader view.

They may see:

• The picture of the room where someone who is talking's story takes place

• A presence standing just outside the frame, connected to what the photo does not show

• A scene playing in their mind that happened just before or just after the captured moment

> *"This hallway looks clean, but I see a woman crying in the far corner. She was just out of frame when this picture was taken."*
> *"There's nothing in this still, but in my mind, I see the child backing away, slowly. He was scared."*

OS Clairvoyant Echoseer

(Over Sensitive - Sensitivity 10)

The OS Clairvoyant Echoseer is flooded with broad, immersive psychic vision. They don't imagine. They enter the visual field and are pulled into panoramic memory, often with intense emotional resonance and disorientation. Sometimes, this forces them into a trance, where they lose their actual vision, and what they receive psychically takes over.

They do not receive close-ups unless they are also a Lenseborn. They may see a field, but not the inscription on the gravestone. They may see the argument that happened before an event, but not the facial hair or color of a shirt.

Untrained, OS Echoseers may:
- Have difficulty distinguishing what is in front of them and what is being psychically retrieved
- Will lose their eyesight and see instead a vision (ambulomancy)
- Get stuck in looped echoes of events, especially violent, traumatic, or grief-heavy imagery, unable to stop the visions

Trained, however, they become panoramic truth-holders, able to read the emotional and psychic climate of any captured moment, not by zooming in, but by standing in what was left out.

They may:

• Suddenly see minutes or hours of psychic footage linked to the event or story
• Be unable to focus on the "main subject" because they are overwhelmed by the ambient, energetic truth of the surroundings.
• Become confused as to what is happening currently in a location vs. a superimposed event that had also happened in the same location.

> *"This video shows them smiling, but I see the hallway. Someone was walking away, there was a fight just before this."*
> *"I can't see inside the car, but the energy around it is tense. Someone's in the trunk. I know it."*

Clairaudient Echoseer

(Regular Sensitivity 6-9)

The regular Clairaudient Echoseer perceives broad, sweeping auditory echoes of thoughts, conversations, and sounds. These impressions do not override their physical hearing, meaning they can still hear the environment around them, but the psychic sense occurs distantly or within their mind. People hear in their heads. If I say, "Hit me with your best shot," some of you will hear the song start to play with her voice. You've had songs in your head, or conversations play out in your mind. Hearing voices in your head is no longer a determining factor for mental illness. The Echoseer might hear sounds from the past or present.

Their auditory impressions are broad, like watching a film or story unfold, but they cannot zoom in on fine details. They receive a field perception, not exact specifics.

Echoseers are especially valuable when:
- Hearing the background energy of spaces, people, or events that have left emotional traces, without being able to focus on the finer details.

- They may hear songs play as part of a movie soundtrack in order to give meaning to what had happened during an event.

CLAIRAUDIENT ECHOSEER

They may hear:

- Fragments of conversations that have occurred in the past, but the psychic voice feels distant, like listening to a recording from another room.

- Ambient sounds from past moments, like distant crying or laughter that occurred during an event.

- Echoes of music or sounds from significant moments, but these sounds are not felt in their environment; they occur in their mind's ear.

> *"I hear voices in the distance, but they don't feel here. It's as if they're from a different time, but I know they belong to this space." "The music is faint in my mind, but I hear a clash before the laughter begins."*

OS Clairaudient Echoseer

(Over Sensitive - Sensitivity 10)

The Over Sensitive Clairaudient Echoseer experiences the psychic sense as an override to their own physical hearing. This means they lose access to their own environment's sounds as their mind is flooded with intense, broad auditory impressions. They become overwhelmed by the stories they perceive, often to the point where their physical hearing is blocked out, and they are immersed in the psychic auditory experience. They can't tell the difference between what is occurring with sound waves and what is occurring in their mind.

Trained, they become panoramic truth-holders, able to hear what has happened or is happening in a location or event through the auditory energy.

Untrained, they may:

- Lose the ability to distinguish between what they hear psychically and the physical world around them.

- Be pulled into trance states where they are caught in the loop of the echoes, unable to hear the current environment.

- Feel physically disoriented, unable to differentiate between past and present sounds, leading to overwhelm.

They may hear:

- Full conversations or sounds from an earlier time, but these sounds take over their physical sense of hearing.

- Auditory energy that feels immersive, like stepping into an event and hearing repeating snippets or fragmented voices, while the sounds in the physical world are also playing.

- Environmental sounds from the past or future, such as cries, music, or whispers, and they can't separate the psychic impression from the present.

> *"Do you hear those people arguing? It sounds like it is coming from upstairs. What do you mean no one lives there?"*
> *"Who is playing music right now? It's midnight! No one? Odd. It's actually the perfect song for this situation... like someone is playing a soundtrack to what you are talking about."*

Claircognizant Echoseer

(Regular Sensitivity 6-9)

The regular Claircognizant Echoseer knows the broad, sweeping images and emotions tied to a place, event, or object. Instead of seeing or hearing the events unfold, they just know what is associated with the space or memory they are perceiving. They understand the event that took place.

They experience this knowing as thoughts or impressions that arise when they come into contact with a place, object, or person, and they don't need to see or hear the specifics. It is a form of psychic knowledge tied to emotional resonance and psychic memory.

The Claircognizant Echoseer can describe many elements of an event like they are recalling a picture or something they once saw themselves. Their ability to name environmental factors, how many people were present, and the general aspects of the event from which they are receiving the electromagnetic energy is unmatched.

CLAIRCOGNIZANT ECHOSEER

They know:

- The emotion that was left in a room, like knowing a room was filled with joy or despair before they entered, without needing to witness it directly.

- The general history or story behind a place, such as knowing that a building was once a family home but later became the site of a tragedy.

- They know that someone's favorite memory was a time their grandmother took them to a park with the ocean breeze and crust-cut sandwiches on a grassy hill.

> *"This is where she hid the slaves... this grave yard. She handed them off from the freedom trail here."*
> *"He signed the papers in this room, on a Tuesday in the middle of winter with the window open."*

OS Claircognizant Echoseer

(Over Sensitive - Sensitivity 10)

The Over Sensitive Claircognizant Echoseer experiences a stronger, overwhelming knowing of spaces, people, and events, as if they are their own memories. Their knowing overrides their physical senses, meaning they might lose awareness of the present moment as they are flooded with intuitive impressions of what has happened or will happen. The information they receive is panoramic and can be so intense that it may lead them to experience trance-like states or disorientation, or they may confuse knowing about an event with having a memory of it (since they have not actually experienced what they are sensing).

Trained, they become highly attuned to the energetic and emotional imprints of spaces, able to sense the deeper truths of events, using their "knowing" to help uncover the broader story without needing the specifics.

Untrained, they may:
- Lose their physical focus of their mind because they are overloaded with information, to the point where they cannot differentiate between their physical surroundings and the psychic impressions they are receiving.

- Confuse their memories with someone else's.

OS CLAIRCOGNIZANT ECHOSEER

They know:

- The emotional landscape of a space, such as immediately knowing that a place was filled with anger, grief, or joy, but with no need for detailed perception.

- The story of a location or person in broad strokes, like knowing how a person was murdered.

- Knowing what happens at the end of the movie as if they already watched it.

> *"I know how it ended the moment I stepped in. I don't need to see the rest, the whole story just landed in me like it was already mine."*
>
> *"Sometimes I can't tell if it's my memory or someone else's. I walk into a place, and suddenly, I remember things I never lived. Like more than de ja vu."*

Clairsentient Echoseer

(Regular Sensitivity 6-9)

The regular Clairsentient Echoseer perceives an emotional feeling and physical sensation of places, events, and moments. They experience the energy of a space or event through their body, feeling the emotional residue or physical discomfort that remains.

These impressions are broad and environmental, and the Clairsentient Echoseer does not need fine details to interpret the emotional or physical energy around them. They might feel the weight of a memory left behind, like sweat on their palms from someone who had been anxious in the same location, or the chill on their neck where a terrifying event occurred.

They may also wake up suddenly feeling the societal dread of a location because of a mass tragedy happening somewhere else in the world. Feeling the intense emotions or strife from an event may overwhelm a regular Clairsentient Echoseer's senses.

They feel:
- The emotional undertones of a location, such as sadness, joy, or fear, without seeing or hearing any specific details. For example, they may feel lingering grief in one room or lightness and hope in another.

- Physical sensations mirror what others have experienced, like feeling a tightness in their chest when someone has experienced anxiety or pain in their legs when someone was physically injured in that space.

- Energy flows from objects or people, picking up sensations of connection or disconnection that leave an emotional or physical imprint on their bodies.

> *"I don't need to know what happened. I can feel the fear clinging to the walls like smoke that never cleared."*
> *"The room feels heavy, like someone cried here and the sadness never left. It's still sitting in the air."*

OS Clairsentient Echoseer
(Over Sensitive - Sensitivity 10)

The Over Sensitive Clairsentient Echoseer experiences extreme emotional and physical sensations that override their normal physical senses. These sensations are so intense that they can manifest directly on their skin, mimicking wounds, discomforts, or emotional turmoil from the past. When in close proximity to an emotionally charged location or event, or even while someone is retelling a story, their physical body can react as though it is directly experiencing what occurred, creating a powerful empathic overload.

Trained, they become attuned to the energy imprints left behind, able to interpret the emotional and physical sensations around them to uncover the deeper truth or emotional history without being overwhelmed.

Untrained, they may:

- Physically collapse or become disoriented when flooded by ANY energy from a location, event, or person, unable to differentiate their own feelings from the psychic impressions they are receiving.

- They are overloaded by sensations, unable to focus on the present moment due to the overwhelming emotional or physical sensations they are experiencing.

They feel:

- Physical wounds or injuries that appear on their own body. For example, they might feel or show the exact cut, bruise, or strain someone experienced when they are standing in the same place where the event occurred.

- Physical discomforts or emotions such as coldness, pressure, or heat, which they experience as echoes of what others felt in the past, like feeling the suffocating pressure someone felt during a panic attack.

> *"Catch me, I'm going to faint."*
> *"I walked into the room and my ribs started aching. I didn't see what happened here, but my body remembers for them."*
> *"Sometimes the grief hits so hard I can't breathe, and I don't even know whose it is. I just know it was left behind."*

Clairgustant Echoseer

(Regular Sensitivity 6-9)

The regular Clairgustant Echoseer perceives broad, sweeping taste impressions tied to events, people, or locations. These taste impressions are not symbolic or metaphorical, but literal sensations of flavor or texture that reflect the emotional and energetic residue left behind.

The Clairgustant's impressions are often linked to what was experienced in the space, such as the bitterness of conflict or the sweetness of joy. These impressions appear as flavors or tastes in the mouth that reveal the underlying emotional or psychic state of a past event or present interaction.

These flavors are not specific to food, but tied to energetic tastes, giving the Echoseer a unique perspective on events or spaces, by experiencing them through the medium of taste.

CLAIRGUSTANT ECHOSEER

They taste:

- The flavor of emotional conflict, such as the sourness or sharp bitterness of anger, sorrow, or guilt left behind in a location or event.

- The sweetness or smoothness of happiness, fulfillment, or peace, sometimes tasting sugar, honey, or even fruit, when the energy in a space is light and free.

- The residue of past experiences, where food-related tastes evoke the emotions attached to a situation or place.

"I walked in and it hit me... bitter, like burnt coffee and regret. What you told me about the case, well it ended in turmoil and was a precise happening."

"There's a sweetness on my tongue, like honey... someone loved deeply in this place, and it's still lingering."

OS Clairgustant Echoseer
(Over Sensitive - Sensitivity 10)

The Over Sensitive Clairgustant Echoseer experiences taste impressions in an overwhelming and intense way that overrides their normal physical sense of taste. These impressions are incredibly vivid and immediate, taking over their mouth and throat and sometimes extending to their entire body. The sensations are so intense that they may feel as though they are reliving the emotions or events through the taste itself, sometimes even to the point of becoming physically ill.

Trained, they become attuned to energetic flavors, able to sense the emotional state of a person or location through the psychic taste, helping them uncover hidden truths, deep emotional wounds, or powerful shifts in energy, all through the flavorful impressions they receive.

Untrained, they may:
- Struggle with intense sensory overload, as they cannot differentiate between the psychic impressions and their physical sense of taste. They may even gag or vomit if the sensations are too strong or overwhelming.

- Feel physically drained or fatigued after experiencing overwhelming tastes tied to psychic imprints, as the body and senses try to process the intensity of the event's residue.

They taste:

- Flavors are linked to the trauma or experiences of others, such as metallic blood, sourness, or burnt food when connected to violent or stressful events.

- The richness of joy or fulfillment through the taste of sweet foods, chocolate, or spices when reflecting on happy or peaceful moments.

- Sharp, off-putting tastes like nails on a chalkboard, acidity bitterness, or chemical tastes when the energy around them feels off, dangerous, or emotionally overwhelming.

> *"It tasted like metal and ash... guilt still clings to the air, even if no one speaks of it."*
> *"I caught a trace of vanilla and mint... whoever was here likes to chew gum."*

Clairalient Echoseer

(Regular Sensitivity 6-9)

The regular Clairalient Echoseer perceives broad, environmental olfactory impressions tied to events, people, or spaces. The literal smells that arise psychically and reflect the emotional or energetic memory of a moment are whiffs of energy instead of scents. Their impressions are immersive, sensory echoes... not fine-tuned or specific, but sweeping and atmospheric. The scent impressions arrive spontaneously, often tied to an event's emotional climate or the unresolved psychic weight of a space.

These scents are broad and emotionally anchored, not forensic or sharply detailed. A Clairalient Echoseer cannot tell you the brand of perfume or the name of a chemical... but they can tell you what the space remembers, what emotions are held there, and what type of story unfolded based on the lingering psychic scent.

CLAIRALIENT ECHOSEER

They smell:

- The psychic residue of conflict, such as the acrid tang of smoke, metallic sharpness, or the mustiness of decay... signaling anger, grief, or trauma that has lingered in the environment.

- The scents of warmth or peace, like clean linen, rain on earth, or fresh citrus—impressions left behind by joy, love, or personal breakthrough.

- Environmental echoes, such as sterile alcohol from a hospital room where a passing occurred... or the cloying sweetness of perfume in a space where someone died but didn't want to be forgotten.

> *"The moment I stepped inside, I smelled copper and burnt wax... there was violence here, and something spiritual was severed when it happened."*
>
> *"It smells like citrus and warm sun in here... like someone finally forgave themselves and walked away free."*

OS Clairalient Echoseer

(Over Sensitive – Sensitivity 10)

The Over Sensitive Clairalient Echoseer is flooded with immersive, involuntary psychic smells that override their physical sense of smell. They don't imagine... they inhale. These intense olfactory visions often sweep in without warning and can disorient the Echoseer's connection to the present moment. Their system does not distinguish between what is physically present and what is psychically retrieved. When they enter a place, speak with someone, or watch a story unfold, their body breathes in the emotional residue left behind.

Unlike their regular counterparts, OS Clairalient Echoseers cannot always pull out of the experience. The scent may remain long after they've left the place. In extreme cases, it may even appear as a phantom smell that haunts them, especially when the energy they encountered remains unresolved. Without training, they may lose the ability to tell which smells are "real" and which are psychic. This confusion can be emotionally and physically overwhelming.

Trained, however, they become scent-based oracles... able to interpret the emotional atmosphere of past events with depth and accuracy, using their nose to walk through memory itself.

They smell:

- The scent of an event as if it is physically present, like smoke, blood, rot, or rust, manifesting in the air with such clarity that the OS Echoseer may gag, recoil, or become dizzy.

- The sharp sweetness of grief, like wilted flowers or spilled wine. Emotions left unresolved that cling to doorways and floors, no longer visible but still scenting the energetic air.

- The heaviness of spiritual unrest, such as waxy incense mixed with sweat or the burning edge of metal, signaling that what happened in the space was both sacred and broken.

> *"It's not here now, but I can still smell it... sulfur and wet wool. Someone summoned something they couldn't control, and it left its stink in the walls."*
>
> *"This isn't your perfume... it's hers. The one who died here. She hasn't left, and she wants you to remember her."*

5s: Bondreaders

Relationships

They see what holds us together, and what quietly pulls us apart. The Bondreader is a psychic attuned to the threads of connection between people, objects, places, and events. These are not always visible ties, but energetic bonds; felt, formed, strained, or broken. Where others sense a mood, the Bondreader senses a structure, a flow of energy and emotion that passes between things, even in silence.

They perceive the direction of connection: who gives, who takes, where energy is blocked, and where it drains away. A healthy bond hums with reciprocity. A damaged thread pulses with imbalance. And the Bondreader feels, sees, or knows it all. In relationships, they know what is true and what is needed. In places, they can feel what has been left behind. They are especially skilled in recognizing imbalanced ties like codependency, obsession, energetic vampirism, and long before they manifest in words or action.

Bondreaders may not know the details of how people met or why they stay, but they know what holds. They can tell you if a connection heals or harms, sustains or drains. In this way, they are quiet architects of truth, not telling you what to choose, only revealing what you're already woven into.

5S: BONDREADERS

> *The Bondreader doesn't ask who you love. They show you where your energy goes.*
> *Every connection speaks. They simply listen.*

Clairvoyant Bondreader

(Regular Sensitivity 6-9)

The regular Clairvoyant Bondreader sees in their mind's eye the energetic cords that connect people to each other, to places, objects, or moments in time. These cords are literal energy lines, reflecting the health, intention, and current state of the connection.

These cords do not lie. They may contradict how a person describes a relationship, showing emotional dissonance, betrayal, or emotional starvation even if the sitter believes the bond is stable.

This information helps people understand how they feel and how they are actually exchanging energy.

They may see in their mind:
- A bright, strong cord glowing between two partners, indicating healthy attachment
- A frayed, unraveling thread between a person and their career, showing burnout or misalignment
- A cord with parasites or black sludge, indicating toxic energetic entanglement, manipulation, or trauma

They can also:
- See how energy moves between people (who gives, who takes)
- Identify imbalances, codependency, or spiritual cord abuse
- Determine if a connection is reciprocal, one-sided, starving, or severed

> *"You say you're close to your sister, but your cords are thinning. You're holding on... she's already pulling away."*
>
> *"There's something feeding on the line between you and that house. It's not just nostalgia... it's an energetic attachment that's draining you."*

OS Clairvoyant Bondreader

(Over Sensitive - Sensitivity 10)

The OS Clairvoyant Bondreader doesn't see cords in their mind; they see them with their physical eyes, layered over reality like threads of light, shadows, or living filaments that stretch from person to person, object to body, or place to memory.

To them, these cords look real, like veins of light, webs, smoke trails, wires, or strands of shadow, and often stretch in all directions. They may see connections across great distances, through walls, or even between timelines (as in connections to others from past lives).

Untrained, they may:
- Struggle to focus in public due to sensory overload
- Feel emotionally or physically impacted by cords breaking, constricting, or decaying
- Mistake psychic cords for actual visual hallucinations, especially if their Clairvoyance is untreated or misunderstood

Trained, they become psychic surgeons of energetic relationships, able to assess, describe, and even assist in clearing, healing, or severing cords with clarity and precision.

OS CLAIRVOYANT BONDREADER

They may see:
- Glowing, pulsing cords that ripple with movement, signaling harmony and exchange
- Tight, twisted cords wrapped around someone's throat, legs, or heart, symbolizing energy that controls or restricts
- Snapping cords, mid-conversation, as someone energetically detaches in real-time
- Disintegrating or webbed cords, indicating spiritual parasites, energetic debt, or emotional entrapment

> *"That man sitting across from you? There's a cord from him to your root chakra. It's red and pulsing. He's taking from you sexually. Did you sleep with him?"*
>
> *"You still have a golden thread to your childhood home. It's thin, but it's there. That's where your peace lives."*

Clairaudient Bondreader
(Regular Sensitivity 6-9)

The regular Clairaudient Bondreader receives psychic information through clear hearing, not of random noise, but of the energetic movement and condition of a relationship or bond. They may hear tones, tension, music, words, or movement that reflect the health, direction, or distortion of a connection.

They may also hear phrases that reveal energetic truths, spoken in the mind's ear or in the voice of someone connected to the relationship. Their gift allows them to hear the current flow of energy in a relationship.

They might hear in their mind:
- A tight buzzing when a relationship is strained or misaligned
- A slow, rhythmic hum when the energy between two people is healthy and reciprocal
- Static, silence, or screeching when someone has gone emotionally or spiritually numb

CLAIRAUDIENT BONDREADER

They are especially gifted at detecting:
- Imbalance (when one person is giving more than the other)
- Unspoken emotional conflict through tone or tension
- When a person is withholding or energetically withdrawing, even if they say otherwise

> ***"She's not listening."***
> ***"You don't belong here anymore."***
> ***"Why are you still feeding this?"***

OS Clairaudient Bondreader

(Over Sensitive - Sensitivity 10)

The OS Clairaudient Bondreader hears energetic relationship dynamics as if they were real, external sounds. Their brain doesn't distinguish between physical and psychic audio, meaning they may hear relationship echoes out loud, in layered voices, melodic tones, or even overlapping dialogues, especially when near people who are deeply bonded, emotionally volatile, or secretly entangled.

In some cases, they may overhear literal emotional truths being "spoken" psychically by one party in a bond, even if the person isn't physically present.

Trained, OS Clairaudient Bondreaders can diagnose the emotional and energetic condition of a relationship with eerie precision. They hear the pull, the decay, the hunger, and the harmony without needing to witness any outward expression.

Untrained, they may:
- Misattribute others' energetic thoughts as their own
- Be overwhelmed in public spaces where multiple relationships are active or volatile
- Assume they're "losing it" when they hear cords snapping or feel a sudden sound drop in a quiet room

They might hear:
* Chains dragging or cords tightening when someone is in a controlling or codependent dynamic
* A chorus of conflicting voices when two people are bonded but deeply divided
* Silence or fading music when someone is emotionally or spiritually exiting a relationship

> *"I hear her voice saying, 'It's not enough anymore.' That's the energy running between you."*
> *"You keep telling yourself you're over him, but the cord still sings when I say his name."*
> *"I hear, 'I still love you', 'This is dying', and 'Take what you want from me,' with my real hearing as you talk about him."*

Claircognizant Bondreader

(Regular Sensitivity 6-9)

The regular Claircognizant Bondreader has the immediate and undeniable knowledge of the truth, quality, and nature of a connection between people, people and places, people and objects, or even a person and a specific timeline, event, or choice. This knowledge is not speculative or symbolic. It is clear, direct, and unshakable.

They don't see the cords. They don't feel them. They don't hear them. They just know.

The emotions of a situation do not guide them. They are guided by energetic certainty.

They may instantly know:
- That a romantic relationship is one-sided or already spiritually severed
- That a person is still deeply tied to their ex-partner, regardless of what they claim
- That a person's connection to their childhood home is parasitic, nurturing, or unfinished

They are especially powerful when:
- A client is confused or in denial about the reality of a bond
- A connection is emotionally charged or masked by attachment
- A decision needs to be made about cutting or continuing a relationship or commitment

> *"You're not in love. You're emotionally dependent."*
> *"He's already gone, even if his body's still there."*
> *"You'll never be at peace until you go back and finish what happened in that house."*

OS Claircognizant Bondreader

(Over Sensitive - Sensitivity 10)

The OS Claircognizant Bondreader doesn't just know what's true about a bond. They download the entire dynamic in a flash of complete psychic clarity. Their system absorbs the structure of the relationship instantly; its history, its present energy flow, its direction, and its potential fracture points. It hits all at once. And it's rarely wrong.

Because the knowing is so total, OS Cognizant Bondreaders can be emotionally affected or overwhelmed if untrained. They may speak with brutal clarity and unintentionally trigger sitters, confuse the knowledge with judgment or personal bias if emotionally entangled, and/or struggle to explain their knowing without appearing arrogant or harsh.

Trained, they become living declarations of truth. Their role is not to feel it, see it, or unravel it. It is to know it. Say it. Name it. With authority.

These downloads may include:
- Phrases like, "She'll leave when the debt is paid."
- "This bond was formed in survival, not love."
- "This house is still feeding on you."

They may:

- Know whether a relationship is transactional or predatory within seconds of meeting the people involved
- Understand how one partner manipulates the other emotionally or energetically
- Be confident of who gives, who takes, and what karmic or spiritual contract is being played out, without hearing a word

> *"You already broke this cord when he cheated. You're just pretending it's still there."*
> *"This connection doesn't serve you. It consumes you. And you know that, or you wouldn't be here."*

Clairsentient Bondreader

(Regular Sensitivity 6-9)

The regular Clairsentient Bondreader feels the emotional and energetic dynamic of a connection in their own body. Their nervous system acts as a tuning fork, reacting to the quality and flow of energy between people, or between a person and a place, object, or event.

These psychics are extremely useful when a client can't articulate what they're feeling. The Bondreader will feel it for them, and reflect it back with clarity.

Their body tells them how energy is moving in the relationship:
- Is it flowing or blocked?
- Is it balanced or one-sided?
- Is it safe, charged, starving, or parasitic?

CLAIRSENTIENT BONDREADER

They may:

- Feel lightness, warmth, and fullness when a bond is healthy and reciprocal
- Experience nausea, pressure, or collapse when a relationship is draining, coercive, or breaking
- Detect a magnetized pull toward a person or place that is significant, even across distance or time

> *"Every time you talk about her, I feel heaviness in my chest. That's not love... it's obligation."*
>
> *"When you mention that city, my whole body warms. You're still connected to it, and it still feeds you."*

OS Clairsentient Bondreader
(Over Sensitive - Sensitivity 10)

The OS Clairsentient Bondreader experiences direct embodiment of the energy moving between others. They may feel as if they are inside the connection, feeling everything from both ends at once. Their body reacts viscerally and often uncontrollably when cords are activated, strained, or corrupted.

Because they feel both sides of a connection, they often understand more about what's happening than the people involved do. Their system overrides social performance and reports only energetic truth.

Untrained, they may:
- Confuse their own emotions with the ones they're absorbing
- Feel overwhelmed in crowded or emotionally tense environments
- Become physically ill from overexposure to cords that are toxic or heavily distorted

Trained, however, OS Clairsentient Bondreaders become walking instruments of energetic accuracy. They feel what's true, and they can tell when a bond is healing, dying, or killing someone.

They may:

• Feel literally pulled toward someone across a room by an energetic thread
• Experience stomach cramps, chest pressure, sexual arousal, or full-body numbness when tuning into emotionally charged or trauma-laced cords
• Mirror the emotional state of the person someone is bonded to, even if that person isn't physically present

> *"Your partner may say he's fine, but when you say his name, I feel like vomiting. That's his energy leaking through your cord."*
>
> *"You think you're done with her, but I can feel the heat between you like it's mine. That cord is still alive... and it's starving."*

Clairgustant Bondreader
(Regular Sensitivity 6-9)

The regular Clairgustant Bondreader receives distinct taste impressions when they tune into a relationship or energetic connection. The taste is not metaphorical: It is a psychic reaction to the energetic flavor of that bond. Every relationship has an energetic composition, and these psychics interpret it through their mouths.

They can taste the direction of energy (giving vs. taking). Whether a cord is nutritive, draining, balanced, or venomous will also manifest into a taste. If something that seems good is actually sour beneath the surface, you will experience it.

Clairgustant Bondreaders are excellent at showing clients where they're feeding energy into something that no longer feeds back, and when they're mistaking hunger for connection.

They may taste:

• Honey, wine, or fresh fruit when a bond is mutually nourishing or romantic

• Metal, mold, or ash when a connection is one-sided, decaying, or parasitic

• Dryness or bitterness when the relationship is emotionally empty, starved, or breaking

> *"Your relationship tastes like fermented fruit, sweet, but overripe. Something's turning."*
> *"When you mention your old apartment, my mouth fills with smoke. That place still holds something toxic."*

OS Clairgustant Bondreader

(Over Sensitive - Sensitivity 10)

The OS Clairgustant Bondreader doesn't just get taste impressions: they experience intense, uncontrollable flavor responses in real-time. Their mouth may fill with taste the moment they walk into a room with active cords, or when someone mentions a person or place they're bonded to. Their body is constantly ingesting psychic residue from connections, especially unspoken, unresolved, or unhealthy ones.

Untrained, they may:
- Develop food aversions or sudden cravings tied to unresolved energetic bonds
- Lose appetite during sessions or relationships where cords are active
- Mistake psychic taste for health issues, allergies, or psychosomatic responses

Trained, they become energetic connoisseurs, able to describe not just how a bond feels, but what it tastes like, and what that taste says about the quality and integrity of the connection.

They may taste:
- Rotten meat, blood, bile, or bitter alcohol when someone is energetically stuck in an abusive or draining connection
- Ash or burning plastic when cords have been severed violently or manipulatively
- Sugary, cloying sweetness that becomes nauseating when a bond is obsessive, manipulative, or falsely loving

> *"You say she's your best friend, but my mouth fills with bleach every time you mention her. She's feeding on you."*
> *"That house? Tastes like salt and iron. There's grief still sitting in the walls."*

Clairalient Bondreader

(Regular Sensitivity 6-9)

The regular Clairalient Bondreader receives psychic scent impressions when they tune into energetic connections. These smells are not symbolic; they are literal olfactory responses to the current state of an energetic bond. The smell tells them everything: how the energy flows, where it's leaking, and what it's feeding or starving.

They are particularly helpful when assessing long-standing energetic ties that have been unspoken, romanticized, or distorted.

Their scent impressions reveal:
- Whether the energy is mutual or one-sided
- If something is being hidden or rotting under the surface
- When cords are still active even after the relationship ends

They may smell:

- Fresh linen, earth, or floral oils when a connection is balanced, grounded, and nurturing
- Spoiled food, mildew, or stagnant water when energy is clinging, codependent, or unreciprocated
- Burnt sugar, smoke, or rotting wood when energy is toxic, draining, or manipulative

> *"When you mention him, I smell old cologne and mildew. That connection hasn't aged well."*
>
> *"The cord between you and this property smells like soil and cedar; it still grounds you."*

OS Clairalient Bondreader

(Over Sensitive - Sensitivity 10)

The OS Clairalient Bondreader physically smells the energy of relationships and connections, often with overpowering vividness. Their brain does not distinguish between physical and psychic scents. The smell is immediate, intrusive, and unmistakable.

Unlike the regular Clairalient, the OS doesn't just get a whiff, they may be flooded with scent for the duration of the connection, especially if the cords are active, decaying, or unresolved.

Untrained, they may:
• Feel "haunted" by certain smells for hours or days
• Avoid crowds or emotionally charged spaces due to psychic olfactory overload
• Be misdiagnosed with olfactory hallucinations or sensitivities when it is actually pure psychic perception

Trained, OS Clairalient Bondreaders become scent-trackers of energetic truth, able to describe the real smell of a cord's condition, without sugarcoating or filtering.

They may:
- Walk into a room and immediately smell urine, rot, sulfur, perfume, blood, or alcohol, depending on the energy cords present
- Catch the scent of someone's ex or estranged parent simply by proximity to the sitter
- Smell specific scents tied to emotional entrapment, grief, sexual trauma, obsession, or loss

> *"You think you're free of him, but every time you talk about your healing, I smell his cologne. That cord is still wide open."*
>
> *"This house smells like wet dog, vinegar, and ash. Someone suffered here, and that suffering is still connected to the land."*

6s: Veritant

Personality and Essence

Masks are irrelevant. The Veritant sees what remains when performance falls away. Their gift is pure discernment. The ability to perceive a person's core nature, regardless of how it is hidden, curated, or cloaked in charm. Lies do not mislead them. Personas do not impress. They read characters the way others read expressions.

Veritants are often mistaken for intuitives or empaths, but their perception runs deeper. They are not reading emotion; they are reading essence. They can frequently guess, with startling accuracy, someone's zodiac sign, Enneagram type, or behavioral archetype. But more than labels, they understand what drives a person, where their loyalties sit, and what patterns repeat through their relationships and choices.

Many Veritants excel in roles that require truth-seeing: human resources, mediation, negotiation, and justice. They are naturally suited to leadership, but often resist the spotlight, preferring to guide from insight rather than force.

These psychics are amazing at knowing if someone is a good person or not; who to trust and who you should avoid.

Their gift is rarely loud. It whispers. It nudges. But it is nearly always correct.

6S: VERITANT

> *The Veritant does not ask who you say you are. They see who you've always been.*
> *Even if you've spent your whole life hiding, they'll know. And they won't be surprised.*

Clairvoyant Veritant

(Regular Sensitivity 6-9)

The regular Clairvoyant Veritant receives literal visual impressions in their mind's eye that reveal someone's true character or personality architecture. Veritants are not normally Clairvoyant. They are usually Claircognitive, but let's discover those rarities, anyway.

These visions reflect not what someone is becoming, but what someone is. They are static truths, not shifting potentials.

This Clair is especially powerful in HR, therapy, leadership, or any setting where knowing the true nature of someone is more important than what they say or do.

Clairvoyant Veritants can visually identify:
- Core personality types (zodiac, enneagram, etc.), if they are familiar with the model
- Whether someone is fundamentally honest, deceitful, self-serving, compassionate, manipulative, rigid, or open
- The sitter's default behavioral patterns, including how they form relationships, respond to conflict, or hide their weaknesses

They may see:

- A person walking through a maze, indicating someone who thrives on complexity but gets lost in self-made problems
- A person sitting on a throne of glass, suggesting a performative leader with hidden fragility
- The sitter as a child or older version of themselves, depending on which version holds their true core nature

> *"I see you wearing armor made of mirrors. You're not just guarded, you reflect everyone back at themselves so they can't see you."*
>
> *"You appear passive, but I see you planting traps. You never attack directly, but you make sure others fall on their own."*

OS Clairvoyant Veritant

(Over Sensitive - Sensitivity 10)

The OS Clairvoyant Veritant experiences real-time, unfiltered visual projections of a person's essence, often layered over their physical appearance or environment. These visions are so vivid, they can blend with reality, making it difficult to distinguish the person from the vision of who they truly are.

To the OS Clairvoyant Veritant, no one is hidden. Every manipulation, charm, persona, or mask melts away instantly. The truth burns through the performance.

They may see someone smiling sweetly while a vulture stands on their shoulder, or confident speaker who is psychically clutching a tattered security blanket, or a peaceful-looking monk who, energetically, drips with blood and pride.

Untrained, they may:
• Struggle to relate to people because they can't unsee what's beneath the mask
• Mistake these visions as hallucinations or intrusive thoughts
• Become emotionally exhausted or disillusioned from constant exposure to contradictory selves

Trained, they become truth-visionaries, psychic mirrors who reveal not just what someone does, but who they are at their core, and who they have always been.

They may:
• Look at someone and see their face shift into an animal, mask, younger or older version of themselves (hallucination)
• See literal projections of archetypes or traits (a throne, a sword, a child cowering, a wolf, a mimic, a beggar) layered over the person like armor
• Witness who the person becomes in conflict, in private, or in power, regardless of how they present

> *"You keep acting like the victim, but I see the puppet strings in your hand."*
> *"You think you're kind. What I see is a judgment, always measuring, always keeping score."*

Clairaudient Veritant

(Regular Sensitivity 6-9)

The regular Clairaudient Veritant receives literal psychic audio that reveals a person's true nature, motivations, and identity. This may come as internal dialogue, repeated phrases, vocal tones, or psychic commentary that surfaces when the sitter speaks or is being discussed.

These psychics don't expose wounds. They expose core wiring. Their skill is most effective in leadership, conflict resolution, coaching, and any environment where true character matters more than charm.

Clairaudient Veritants are especially gifted at:
- Hearing the discrepancy between what someone says and what they actually believe
- Picking up core beliefs that shape identity, such as pride, entitlement, fear, or insecurity
- Uncovering default internal narratives, such as "I'm the hero," "I'm the victim," or "I'm smarter than everyone else."

They might hear:
- A person says, "I just want peace," while the psychic hears, "I need control."
- A calm voice, but beneath it, a harsher one muttering, "No one's going to take this from me again."
- Their own mind replaying a phrase again and again: "It's always their fault."

> *"You keep saying you're confused, but what I hear is, 'I want someone else to decide for me.'"*
>
> *"You sound calm, but I hear a voice inside repeating, 'No one is better than me.' That's the part you don't let out."*

OS Clairaudient Veritant

(Over Sensitive - Sensitivity 10)

The OS Clairaudient Veritant hears psychic audio layered directly over real-world sound. When someone speaks, the OS Veritant may simultaneously hear the real voice and the authentic voice, the one that reveals the essence. They do not just catch contradictions; they hear what is actually motivating a person, often in a voice tone, language, or rhythm completely different from the one being presented.

Unlike Harrowbinders, who hear shame, or Bondreaders, who hear energetic movement, Veritants hear identity in motion. They do not need proof. The tone is the proof.

Trained, they are infallible discerners of character, capable of hearing the truth even when it is perfectly masked.

Untrained, they may:
- Become overwhelmed by hearing too much psychic content layered over casual speech
- Misidentify psychic hearing as paranoia or inner voices
- Lose trust in surface communication altogether

They may:

• Hear someone say, "It's fine," while simultaneously hearing a second voice scream, "I hate you for this."

• Hear archetypal tones (a king's command, a child's cry, a priest's sermon, a tyrant's threats) embedded within someone's everyday speech

• Be bombarded with overlapping psychic commentary if multiple people are in the room, especially in conflict

> *"You're playing the peacemaker, but I hear the general barking orders underneath."*
> *"He speaks with empathy, but the voice behind it is rehearsed. It says, 'If I say the right things, I stay in control.'"*

Claircognizant Veritant
(Regular Sensitivity 6-9)

The regular Claircognizant Veritant doesn't see, hear, or feel someone's essence. They simply know it. They will say they are just "a good judge of character." Upon meeting someone, or even thinking of them, the Veritant may receive a fully-formed understanding of that person's character, intentions, and internal landscape. This is not judgment. It's not suspicion. It's pure, psychic certainty.

The knowing is immediate, non-negotiable, and often unpopular, because it cuts straight through masks.

Their knowing is more accurate than most people's self-assessment, and often reveals a person's operating system, not just their behavior.

They might instantly know:
- "She lies to avoid conflict."
- "He thrives in chaos and hides behind charm."
- "She wants love, but she needs worship."

Claircognizant Veritants are especially powerful in:
- Group dynamics, where they can name who is truly safe or dangerous
- Interviews, hiring, and leadership, where manipulation or impression management is common
- Interpersonal conflict, where they detect who actually caused the fracture, regardless of who sounds more convincing

> ***"You're not confused. You're stalling. You already know the truth and don't want to say it."***
> ***"He didn't do it to hurt her. He did it to see if she'd leave. That's the pattern."***

OS Claircognizant Veritant

(Over Sensitive - Sensitivity 10)

The OS Claircognizant Veritant experiences total awareness of a person's identity and character, often within seconds of encountering them. It's not a hunch. It's not a guess. It is the full blueprint of who someone is, their archetypal role, emotional drives, blind spots, behavioral defaults, self-deceptions, and hidden strengths.

These downloads are total and overwhelming, often accompanied by a sense of emotional dissonance when the person's behavior contradicts their energetic truth.

Trained, the OS Claircognizant Veritant is one of the most potent psychic diagnosticians of human identity, able to look at someone once and know what would take others years to figure out.

Untrained, they may:

- Struggle to connect with others, because they are always ten steps ahead of surface interactions
- Over-explain or over-analyze themselves to seem more "neutral"
- Be mistaken for arrogant or judgmental when in fact they are simply accurate

They may:

• Know that someone is a chronic victim, a performative empath, or a weaponized nurturer without hearing them speak

• Instantly download a personality type, such as their astrological chart, enneagram profile, or psychological schema, as long as the Veritant is familiar with the system

• Understand exactly how a person will behave under pressure, in love, in conflict, or in leadership, even if that person has never faced those scenarios before

> *"She needs everyone to think she's soft so they won't call out her power games."*
> *"He hasn't said a word, but I know he believes people are either useful or weak. That's who he is."*

Clairsentient Veritant

(Regular Sensitivity 6-9)

The regular Clairsentient Veritant feels a person's essence, integrity, and emotional signature in their own body. They don't need someone to speak or explain. The body tells them everything. The presence of the person triggers an internal response that informs the Veritant who this person truly is.

This Clair is particularly powerful in hiring, partnerships, and leadership roles, anywhere first impressions are carefully curated, but the truth still pulses beneath.

They don't feel others' emotions the way Harrowbinders or Physicians do. Instead, they feel the energetic resonance of personality traits. That includes:

- How someone handles power
- Whether they are honest or performative
- Whether they seek connection, control, or validation

They may feel:
- Tightness in the chest when someone appears kind but is emotionally manipulative
- A sinking in the stomach around someone who wears masks to control others
- A sense of calm strength near someone with deep integrity, even if they speak little

> *"He hasn't done anything wrong, but I feel on guard around him. That means something's off."*
> *"She gives me this cloying, sticky energy. It's like she wants me to like her so badly it makes me want to run."*

OS Clairsentient Veritant

(Over Sensitive – Sensitivity 10)

The OS Clairsentient Veritant embodies the truth of a person's nature in real-time. Their nervous system mirrors not how someone feels, but who they are, and the psychic reaction can be instant, overwhelming, and precise. Their body doesn't just react; it becomes a reflection of the other person's character.

Because the psychic information arrives through the body, they often know who someone is before they speak, just by how their presence hits the system.

Trained, the OS Clairsentient Veritant becomes a living emotional barometer of integrity. They don't listen to words. They listen to how your presence lands in the body, and that tells them everything.

Untrained, they may:
- Misattribute personality reactions as their own trauma responses
- Confuse energetic dishonesty for personal anxiety
- Be accused of being "too sensitive" or "unreasonable" when simply responding to an invisible but real truth

They may:

• Feel their posture shift, mirroring dominance or submission depending on the person they're around

• Experience sudden waves of pride, cowardice, arrogance, or insecurity that belong to the other person, not themselves

• Become physically ill, short of breath, or overstimulated by someone who appears likable but is energetically corrupt

> *"You're trying to be polite, but I feel your disgust like it's mine. That's who you are beneath the performance."*
> *"He smiles and listens, but my body feels like I'm being hunted. That's all I need to know."*

Clairgustant Veritant

(Regular Sensitivity 6-9)

The regular Clairgustant Veritant experiences literal taste impressions in their mouth that reflect the core truth of a person's identity. These flavors are triggered when a person enters their field, speaks, or is the focus of attention. The taste is never random: It represents the energetic signature of the person's character.

They don't need to know the person well. In fact, the less they know, the clearer the taste. Their gift is not about emotions, but the personality truth baked into someone's energy.

This Clair is subtle but sharp. In complex social environments, they act as a psychic taste test for authenticity.

CLAIRGUSTANT VERITANT

They might taste:

• Sugar that sours when someone presents as sweet but is ultimately selfish

• Salt and iron around someone who lives with honor, pain, and duty

• Rot, vinegar, or bile when the person harbors cruelty, superiority, or contempt

> *"He says all the right things, but he leaves the taste of copper and sugar in my mouth. That's usually a narcissist with good PR."*
>
> *"I dont know... he just left a bad taste in my mouth."*

OS CLAIRGUSTANT VERITANT

(OVER SENSITIVE - SENSITIVITY 10)

The OS Clairgustant Veritant receives overpowering flavor downloads tied to the presence or identity of others. Their body fully reacts to the energetic taste of a person's nature, and it can cause physical responses like salivation, dry mouth, nausea, gagging, or cravings.

The taste may change mid-conversation if someone shifts personas, intensify when deception is used to mask the truth, or even show up hours before or after interacting with a person, as a kind of energetic aftertaste.

Trained, the OS Clairgustant Veritant becomes a psychic sommelier of character, able to identify not just a person's outer behavior, but their flavor of soul.

Untrained, they may:
- Struggle to eat around others due to subconscious flavor overlays
- Develop oral fixations, food aversions, or phantom cravings linked to energetic environments
- Be misunderstood as overly picky or sensitive when they're simply tasting the truth

They may:

• Gag when interacting with someone who weaponizes kindness or uses identity to manipulate

• Salivate around someone whose integrity is magnetic, seductive, or pure

• Experience lingering, haunting aftertastes when near deeply deceptive or morally conflicted people

> *"You taste like mold under honey. I don't trust your sweetness."*
> *"She leaves the taste of rain and dark chocolate. Complex. Steady. She's exactly who she says she is."*

Clairalient Veritant

(Regular Sensitivity 6-9)

The regular Clairalient Veritant receives literal psychic scent impressions triggered by a person's presence, name, or image. The smell is how their soul registers to the psychic nose, regardless of how they present.

The smell never lies. It may even contradict everything else the person is saying or doing.

These psychics are especially sharp in spaces where performance is the currency, spiritual spaces, leadership, romance, and politics.

They may smell:
- Old wood, leather, or tobacco around someone grounded, wise, and unmovable
- Bleach, plastic, or artificial floral when someone is constantly masking or performing
- Rot, sulfur, or mildew when the person has a corrupt core or manipulative tendencies

> *"You look polished, but you smell like rust and wet stone.*
> *You've built everything to protect your wounds."*
> *"He's charming, but all I get is bleach and burnt sugar. That's*
> *fake to the bone."*

OS Clairalient Veritant

(Over Sensitive - Sensitivity 10)

The OS Clairalient Veritant smells truth as reality. They don't differentiate between psychic and physical scent. To them, it's just there. A person walks into the room, and suddenly the air smells like copper, lilacs, rotting fruit, gasoline, or baby powder. These scents aren't associated with memory or events. They're associated with essence. Character. Core identity.

These impressions may be overwhelming or cause nausea, migraines, or sensory flooding, lingering for hours after meeting someone, like a spiritual after-scent. Unfortunately, they may have scents that shift abruptly mid-conversation when a person's mask drops or a deeper truth emerges.

Trained, the OS Clairalient Veritant is a psychic bloodhound. They are able to smell the essence of a person and speak it with calm, unwavering accuracy.

Untrained, they may:
- Be unable to tolerate crowded or high-performance spaces
- Misinterpret physical reactions as health issues
- Become emotionally reactive to scent-truth they can't ignore but don't yet understand

They may:
- Smell a person's ego like musk or cloying cologne
- Smell resentment like dried wine and decay
- Smell integrity like cedar, paper, or fresh air

And they may do so before the person even speaks.

> *"Your scent is iron and soap. Clean, but defensive. You've built your life on being good, but never real."*
>
> *"He smells like oak and fire. He doesn't need power. He is power."*

7s: Lenseborns

Details

They are not wide-view seers or dream-readers. The Lenseborn comes into the world with a gift so precise it feels surgical: the ability to zoom in, to see the exact detail that matters most. They perceive the grain of the paper, the shade of a folder, the faded handwriting on a forgotten note. They can describe the texture of an object they've never touched, or give a string of lottery numbers with startling specificity, not because they see the future, but because they see exactly what is.

Their perception is not broad; it is focused. Intensely so. Like a magnifying glass held to the fabric of the moment, the Lenseborn extracts truth in high resolution. Every psychic sense tightens around a pinpoint of meaning: a smell, a word, a flash of color. Clarity doesn't come in waves; it comes in needles.

Because of this, Lenseborns often miss the bigger picture. They don't track the room. They track the corner of the envelope on the table. But within that corner may be the key to everything. They are not built to generalize or feel emotional flow. Their gift is microscopic certainty, and they wield it like a blade.

7S: LENSEBORNS

The Lenseborn doesn't tell you what's coming. They tell you the date on the torn ticket in your coat pocket.
They see what others overlook... and only that.

Clairvoyant Lenseborn

(Regular Sensitivity 6-9)

The regular Clairvoyant Lenseborn receives visual psychic information with uncanny specificity. Their visions are zoomed-in, detail-rich, and often obsessive in clarity. When they connect, their Clairvoyance ignores the "big picture" and dives directly into a single visual element that holds significance.

They do not see context. They often cannot tell you where the item is or what it means outside the visual unless another archetype is also active. Their job is to see clearly and name the details exactly.

They are ideal for:
- Missing persons cases
- Object location
- Psychic profiling, when someone needs specifics instead of generalities

They may see:

- A red folder on a desk, with a gold-embossed emblem and a missing corner
- A locket hidden in drywall, its chain rusted, the initials etched faintly into the back
- A barcode, serial number, or lottery ticket, but only if that detail is within their energetic access

> *"I don't know why this matters, but I see a green lighter with chipped paint and a flame that stutters."*
> *"There's a cracked window pane. Lower right. One streak of dried blood... horizontal."*

OS Clairvoyant Lenseborn

(Over Sensitive - Sensitivity 10)

The OS Clairvoyant Lenseborn sees psychic detail layered over the physical world, often without warning and with intrusive clarity. Their eyes may physically twitch, their gaze may fixate, or their mind may become consumed by a single specific object or detail, regardless of its larger context.

To them, it's not "a vision." It's an ocular reality. They don't imagine. They observe, with laser focus. And what they focus on is never random. It always holds psychic relevance.

Untrained, they may:
- Lose awareness of surroundings while visually locked onto psychic detail
- Be misdiagnosed with attention or sensory disorders
- Experience eye strain, mental fatigue, or intrusive visual overlays

Trained, the OS Clairvoyant Lenseborn becomes an elite psychic investigator, able to retrieve evidence-level visual data from psychic space.

They may:

- See numbers on the wall where nothing is written
- Fixate on a person's shoelace, knowing something happened during the tying
- Be unable to look away from a smudge on a mirror, because it holds energetic residue no one else perceives

> *"The woman is wearing a navy blazer. There's a pin missing from the left lapel. It was removed... intentionally."*
> *"There's a broken tile behind the toilet. Fourth one up. There's something hidden there."*

Clairaudient Lenseborn

(Regular Sensitivity 6-9)

The regular Clairaudient Lenseborn receives precise, auditory psychic input, often single words, syllables, repeated fragments, or isolated sounds. What they hear is not symbolic. It is exact. It might be meaningless to others, but to the psychic, it's the key in the lock.

Their gift is not about ambiance, emotion, or atmosphere; it's about precision.

They excel when asked to:
- Pinpoint when the lie was told
- Identify what word triggered the shift
- Retrieve auditory evidence psychically, like hearing what was actually said in a past conversation

They may:
- Hear a single name repeated, even if it's whispered or unspoken
- Catch one word that keeps echoing during a session, often the most important
- Pick up a tiny sound: a creak, click, tear, breath, or laugh, and know that's where the truth lives

> *"I keep hearing 'check,' like a checkmark. Not money. Just that word."*
> *"Someone keeps whispering 'five.' I don't know what it means, but it won't stop."*
> *"There's a sound... like scissors closing. That's where the memory cuts off."*

OS Clairaudient Lenseborn

(Over Sensitive - Sensitivity 10)

The OS Clairaudient Lenseborn hears psychic sounds with sensory precision, often layered over real-world sound or playing on repeat in the mind. They do not hear voices in a vague, conversational sense. They hear micro-clips: sharp, clear, and often obsessive fragments.

For them, the sound isn't "subtle." It is piercing, obvious, and often invasive, a thread that must be followed until it is resolved.

Untrained, they may:
- Be misdiagnosed with OCD or auditory hallucinations
- Feel haunted by meaningless snippets of speech or song
- Struggle to focus if the psychic sound is stuck or looping

Trained, they are the forensics team of psychic sound, able to name the exact phrase, exact tone, or exact trigger word with surgical clarity.

They may:

- Hear a tone shift no one else registers, and know that's where it changed
- Fixate on a single lyric, syllable, or sound, even if no one else can hear it
- Become overwhelmed by the internal repetition of a psychic sound or phrase until it is acknowledged or spoken aloud

> *"The argument wasn't about the dishes. It was when she said, 'Just like your mother.' That was the snap."*
>
> *"The man didn't yell. He whispered, 'Run.' I heard it. That's what saved her."*

Claircognizant Lenseborn

(Regular Sensitivity 6-9)

The regular Claircognizant Lenseborn receives specific psychic information as a sudden, total download, but unlike other Claircognizants, they do not receive emotional truths or general insights. They receive answers.

They excel in missing person cases, technical psychic work (codes, locks, machines), and competitive or test-based divination scenarios (lotto numbers, tests, elections, etc.).

Their information is singular and sharp, often appearing as:
- A number, word, phrase, or password
- A correction to a guess someone else made
- A code, frequency, or item that seems out of context, but proves to be accurate

CLAIRCOGNIZANT LENSEBORN

They might:
- Instantly know a PIN number, locker combination, or street address
- Say the correct name of a person they've never met
- Know the exact date something happened (or will happen) without knowing why

> *"Her name was Elise. I don't know how I know that... it's just true."*
> *"You'll find the ring in box 148."*
> *"It's 3:41 p.m. That's when it happened."*

OS Claircognizant Lenseborn

(Over Sensitive - Sensitivity 10)

The OS Claircognizant Lenseborn receives rapid-fire, involuntary psychic data with such specificity that it often feels invasive or too "on the nose." They don't interpret information. They become the answer. It's not about confidence. It's about certainty that overrides logic.

The knowing comes in flashes, often without explanation, and with unshakable confidence, even when it makes no sense at the moment.

Sometimes this can manifest like this: Details of someone whom they are connected to's thoughts will take over the OS Claircognizant Lenseborn's thought pattern, like shopping someone else's grocery list or coming up with an idea that someone else is thinking.

Trained, the OS Claircognizant Lenseborn becomes a psychic code-breaker, able to provide exact pieces of a puzzle with no context and no error.

Untrained, they may:
- Feel isolated because no one believes something so exact could be psychic
- Question their sanity due to the specificity of downloads
- Become overwhelmed by autopilot truths, knowing things before they want to

They may:

- Say a name out loud and then realize it belongs to the person's abuser, ex, or lost loved one
- Know the digits of a phone number or plate number without ever seeing it
- Blurt out information that seems too specific to be psychic, but it is

> *"The password is Sequoia. Lowercase 's.' That's all I got, but I'm sure of it."*
>
> *"Stop looking in October. It happened on September 2nd at 8:16 p.m."*

Clairsentient Lenseborn

(Regular Sensitivity 6-9)

The regular Clairsentient Lenseborn receives exact bodily sensations tied to specific psychic input. Their nervous system pinpoints details. When connecting to a situation or person, their body will mirror the precise location or condition of what needs to be found, healed, or acknowledged.

This precision may also show up in:
- Sensory mimicry (i.e., skin crawling in the exact place an insect was)
- Object location (i.e., body pulling in the direction of a missing item)
- Physical health scanning (down to the tooth, rib, or muscle)

They may:

- Feel a sharp pain in one knuckle and know someone broke their finger
- Experience pinpricks along one thigh and know something is hidden in a pant leg
- Get a tight pressure behind the sternum that only eases once a specific emotion or item is revealed

> *"There's something under your left rib. It's not medical. I just feel pressure there when I'm near you."*
> *"It's in the front coat pocket. My hand burns when you talk about it."*

OS Clairsentient Lenseborn

(Over Sensitive - Sensitivity 10)

The OS Clairsentient Lenseborn experiences acute, involuntary physical mirroring of psychic detail. Their body becomes a map, accurately reproducing everything from pressure, heat, pain, vibration, or density that is tied to a person, object, or space. The information is so exact, it can mimic wounds, ailments, or pressure points with uncanny precision.

They can often walk into a space and physically point to where something is, drop to the floor or double over because of the precise psychic pressure, begin mimicking the very body movement someone else made when an event occurred.

Untrained, they may:
- Be misdiagnosed with sensory or somatic disorders
- Struggle to distinguish psychic sensation from actual injury or illness
- Become physically overwhelmed by too many inputs in a charged location

Trained, they are like psychic MRI machines, capable of identifying energetic abnormalities with exact spatial reference, down to inches, seconds, or body parts.

They may:
- Feel an itch on one knuckle when a buried object is nearby
- Break into a cold sweat across their shoulder blades because a gun was once pointed there
- Experience full-body flinches or muscle twitches tied to an exact moment or item in a location

> *"It's buried under the front right corner of the house. My knees went out when I got close."*
> *"She was shot in the left thigh. That's why I couldn't walk for a second when I touched the photo."*

Clairgustant Lenseborn

(Regular Sensitivity 6-9)

The regular Clairgustant Lenseborn experiences extremely precise psychic taste impressions tied to a person, object, or location. These impressions are not symbolic. They are literal, often pinpointing the material, substance, or contamination connected to the subject. They make great bartenders and chefs.

The taste often comes:
- The moment a person begins speaking
- When holding an object
- When entering a location with psychic weight

Their accuracy lies in naming what's physically present or once was, down to flavor, texture, or contamination.

CLAIRGUSTANT LENSEBORN

They may:
- Taste the poison in something when it has been drugged
- Taste how a cocktail will be without ingesting it
- Taste what to add to a meal without testing it

> *"There's bleach. I taste it. Someone tried to clean something."*
> *"That cake is bad! Don't eat it!"*

OS CLAIRGUSTANT LENSEBORN
(OVER SENSITIVE - SENSITIVITY 10)

The OS Clairgustant Lenseborn receives sudden, invasive, and often overwhelming psychic taste data with total bodily realism. Their mouths may flood with saliva, go dry, burn, or trigger gag reflexes depending on what is psychically "present." The flavor is precise, not interpretive, and can even lead to the identification of unknown substances.

They can identify contaminants in food or water, substances used to bind or bury objects, residual materials left behind after a traumatic event (blood, bile, alcohol, vomit, semen, cleaning fluid).

Trained, they become psychic forensic palates, able to identify what is or was present down to taste, source, and even mixture.

Untrained, they may:
• Avoid eating or drinking due to unpredictable psychic cross-contamination
• Suffer mouth ulcers, acid imbalance, or nausea from intense psychic input
• Struggle to function in unfamiliar spaces until the taste clears

They may:

- Taste the exact chemical makeup of a poisoned drink
- Salivate uncontrollably when describing an item that was hidden near a bakery
- Feel their tongue dry and burn when connecting to desert terrain or spiritual dehydration

> *"It's antifreeze. Sweet but sharp. It was in the drink."*
> *"There's mildew, decaying wood, and salt. The body was near water, maybe under a dock."*

Clairalient Lenseborn

(Regular Sensitivity 6-9)

The regular Clairalient Lenseborn receives specific psychic smell impressions tied to objects, people, and events. Their scent impressions are narrow, detailed, and sharp, often focusing on one ingredient, one compound, or one contaminant.

These smells often:
- Appear suddenly, with no physical source
- Come in short bursts, like a psychic whiff
- Deliver one very precise detail: no more, no less

They are most effective when paired with forensics, missing persons, object location, or energy clearing.

CLAIRALIENT LENSEBORN

They may:

• Smell cigarette ash and hairspray, tied to a person's presence or a crime scene

• Detect the scent of metal, latex, or bleach when describing how something was disposed of or cleaned

• Pick up the scent of dog fur, engine grease, or mildew when a specific person is mentioned

> *"I smell tar and sweat. Whoever touched that item worked in construction."*
> *"It's sweet and moldy. The box was in a cellar for a long time."*

OS Clairalient Lenseborn

(Over Sensitive - Sensitivity 10)

The OS Clairalient Lenseborn receives vivid, full-body scent impressions layered over their actual senses. These psychics cannot distinguish between physical and psychic smell. Their nose fully registers the exact scent of what is psychically present, even if it was there years ago.

What they smell is not faint; they are visceral and intrusive. Often accompanied by emotional or bodily reactions (gagging, sneezing, tears, etc.), many people may think they are behaving out of a need for attention.

Sometimes what they sense is so specific that the OS can name the substance or manufacturer involved.

Untrained, they may:
- Struggle with phantom smells that linger for hours
- Be overwhelmed in crowded spaces with many overlapping energy residues
- Mistake their reactions for allergies or trauma responses

Trained, they become olfactory detectives, able to identify specific materials, trauma signatures, chemical residues, and presences based on smell alone.

They may:

- Smell urine, alcohol, and smoke when entering a room where an event with those smells was present
- Be hit with the scent of a specific brand of cologne tied to an object or deceased person
- Detect bleach and vomit before anyone else notices what happened in a space

> *"He was there. I smell his sweat and the cinnamon gum he always chewed. This is where it happened."*
> *"It's motor oil, fertilizer, and mildew. The object was stored in a toolshed... maybe in a plastic bin."*

PRECOGNITION

HOW THOSE WHO INTUIT THE FUTURE DEMONSTRATE IN THE SEVEN PSYCHIC PATHS ARCHETYPES

Precognition is the ability to psychically access information about future events, whether by vision, sound, knowing, sensation, taste, smell, or energetic impression. However, how this precognitive information comes through varies depending on which Clair a psychic uses and which archetype layer they occupy. This chapter breaks down how precognition appears across every Clair in all seven psychic archetypes, helping you recognize what the future looks like depending on your unique psychic lens.

Thoughts on Precognition:

Precognition doesn't mean prophecy. It's access to future energy, which may or may not solidify into reality. The more grounded and specific the Clair and Archetype, the more measurable and literal the precognition. The deeper the layer, the more complex and emotionally loaded the information.

By studying how you receive the future, you become more accurate, more focused, and more prepared to track patterns in time.

Precognitive Physician

(Surface - Wellness Layer)

Physicians experience precognition by sensing shifts in well-being, safety, or energetic health before they happen. Their future-sight is oriented toward physical, mental, emotional, or spiritual outcomes.

• *Clairvoyant:* May see a client walking with a cane, in a hospital gown, or radiating color changes that reflect illness or recovery that hasn't happened yet.
• *Clairaudient:* Hears hospital sounds, sirens, or a repeating word like "stroke" or "panic" before anything manifests.
• *Claircognizant:* Instantly knows "He will fall ill," or "She will be in recovery soon," even with no outward signs.
• *Clairsentient:* This person feels chest pressure or joint pain in advance, sensing what the client will experience physically or emotionally.
• *Clairgustant:* Tastes dryness, bitterness, or chemical residue, suggesting future medication or internal imbalance.
• *Clairalient:* They smell hospital-grade antiseptic or blood when someone is not yet injured or ill, but will be.

Precognitive Luminator

(Hope & Potential – Aspirational Layer)

Luminators perceive precognitive hope. They see what is possible, not guaranteed, and what future potentials may manifest if the person chooses alignment.

• *Clairvoyant:* Sees the sitter winning awards, standing on a stage, building a family, or living a dream they haven't yet dared to speak aloud.

• *Clairaudient:* Hears an audience clapping, a name being called at a graduation, or a child's laugh, scenes that haven't happened, but could.

• *Claircognizant:* Knows "She will thrive in music," "He was born to teach," even if the sitter has no current plans to pursue these.

• *Clairsentient:* Feels the joy of an unborn child, the peace of future retirement, or the freedom of a decision not yet made.

• *Clairgustant:* Tastes champagne or sweet fruit when a dream is about to be fulfilled, even if the sitter hasn't begun the path.

• *Clairalient:* Smells sunscreen or ocean air when a client will one day live near water, symbolic of their dream life.

Precognitive Harrowbinder

(Shadows & Repression – Deep Fear Layer)

Harrowbinders sense future moments where repressed fears, shame, or desires may come to the surface. Their precognition may be disturbing.

• *Clairvoyant:* Sees a client locked in a bathroom, screaming at a mirror, or seducing someone they haven't met yet, future acts born of hidden desire or trauma.
• *Clairaudient:* Hears a confession, a moan, a threat, or the words "Don't tell anyone," not from the past, but from what will be said.
• *Claircognizant:* Knows "He will cheat," "She will lie," "You will be blamed for something you didn't do." Deep truths are hidden even from the client's conscious self.
• *Clairsentient:* Feels dread in advance of a future moral failure, violent act, or sexual decision the client is headed toward but hasn't yet committed.
• *Clairgustant:* Tastes blood, metal, or spoiled food, often before it manifests in waking life.
• *Clairalient:* Smells rot, smoke, or semen, the future scent of secrets being exposed or acted upon.

Precognitive Echoseer

(Field Echoes – Event Layer)

Echoseers perceive events from the future, especially through video-like visions, events, and mental pictures. Their foresight is often cinematic or picto-graphic.

• *Clairvoyant:* Sees an empty room that will one day be the scene of an event, a party, a murder, or a birth.
• *Clairaudient:* Hears the future audio imprint of laughter, footsteps, or screams before the event occurs.
• *Claircognizant:* Knows what will happen next in a movie.
• *Clairsentient:* Feels anticipation, excitement, dread, or grief about something that hasn't yet happened in a location.
• *Clairgustant:* Tastes champagne because it will be served at an event they are attending later in the week.
• *Clairalient:* Smells future trauma, joy, or chaos in a room where nothing has happened yet, a scent that doesn't match the moment.

Precognitive Bondreader

(Connection & Energy Threads – Relational Layer)

Bondreaders detect the future condition of energetic connections, whether a relationship will grow, die, sever, or become parasitic. They read time by watching how the cords evolve.

- *Clairvoyant:* Sees the thread between two people fraying, tightening, or being cut in the near future, regardless of current appearance.
- *Clairaudient:* Hears a future goodbye, fight, proposal, or a name spoken in longing, revealing how the relationship will unfold.
- *Claircognizant:* Knows "You'll never see him again," or "You'll be family by this time next year," with total certainty.
- *Clairsentient:* Feels hunger, suffocation, warmth, or release from a bond that hasn't yet shifted, feeling what it will become before it arrives.
- *Clairgustant:* Tastes sweetness that turns bitter, or bitterness that becomes nourishing, signaling future relational dynamics.
- *Clairalient:* Smells perfume, rot, or smoke, the future scent of how this relationship will end, evolve, or ignite.

Precognitive Veritant

(Character & Truth – Essence Layer)

Veritants do not just see who someone is now; they may also receive precognitive downloads about who someone will become, or what their character will do in times of stress, temptation, or power.

• *Clairvoyant:* Sees someone transform into a tyrant, healer, or martyr in the future, not symbolically, but literally through future-sight.
• *Clairaudient:* Hears future statements of identity: "I'm not sorry," "This is who I am now," or "I tried to warn you."
• *Claircognizant:* Knows with certainty, "She will betray you," or "He will rise to the challenge, just not yet."
• *Clairsentient:* Feels the tension of a future version of the person, their darker or truer self, long before it emerges.
• *Clairgustant:* Tastes copper or sugar, signaling the personality arc of someone who will sour or sweeten in time.
• *Clairalient:* Smells a future self, the scent of ego, courage, or decay that hasn't manifested yet, but is on the path.

Precognitive Lenseborn

(Precision – Deep Focus Layer)

Lenseborns get pinpointed details of future events: times, codes, colors, smells, items, and physical sensations, all with surgical accuracy. Their precognition is often the most verifiable.

• *Clairvoyant:* Sees the color of the future car, the fold of the document, and the exact location of the key that hasn't yet been hidden.
• *Clairaudient:* Hears the one word that will end the relationship, the exact time someone will arrive, or a phrase that hasn't yet been said.
• *Claircognizant:* Knows lotto numbers, GPS coordinates, passwords, or dates with eerie accuracy, no guessing.
• *Clairsentient:* Feels the pinch, stab, burn, or sensation of something happening in the future, down to the inch.
• *Clairgustant:* Tastes the poison, wine, or metallic blood of a future event, an exact chemical psychic trace.
• *Clairalient:* Smells smoke, gasoline, lilacs, or disinfectant, scents that will be present in a future scene, down to brand or blend.

How This Affects Mediums

Here's a breakdown and definition of each Medium type within the Seven Psychic Paths System, organized clearly so you can reference it. Each type is defined by what kind of non-physical entity or force they communicate with, and how that communication functions.

The word "medium" comes from Latin and means "middle," "intermediary," or "that which conveys." In spiritual and psychic work, a medium serves as a go-between... someone who receives electromagnetic information from a non-physical or unverifiable source and translates it through their psychic senses into something that can be shared with the living.

There are many forms of mediumship, but the most widely recognized is the death medium, someone who receives impressions, messages, or sensations from the human dead. They are called mediums because they exist in the space between what is tangible and what cannot be confirmed through ordinary means. They do not invent the message; they interpret what is received. They are not the source. They are the passageway.

In many cases, the accuracy of the content delivered can be confirmed... names, memories, details, and emotional truths often check out. What cannot be confirmed is the *source* of that information. We cannot prove who or what is speaking. The same is true for mediums who communicate with plants, gods, animals, or entities that affect the physical world. We

HOW THIS AFFECTS MEDIUMS

can validate the message... but not the origin. The medium becomes the intervening point between our senses and something beyond them.

While any Clair and Archetype may appear in any medium, the best fit depends on how the medium connects and what kind of entity or force they're connecting to. By combining mediumship types with the Seven Psychic Archetypes, we gain extraordinary nuance and teachable precision in how spiritual communication actually works.

Death Mediums

Communicates with: Human spirits who have died

Role: The classic medium. These individuals act as bridges between the living and the dead, often relaying messages from departed loved ones.

Clair dominant: Clairaudience, Clairvoyance, Claircognizance, Clairalience

Key feature: Verifiable personal information from deceased people

> *"Your grandmother says the ring is still in the sewing kit."*

Best-suited archetypes:
- 6s – Veritants: Able to pick up the personality of loved ones who have passed on as a form of verification.
- 5s – Bondreaders: Sense the connection from the living and the dead and able to connect to those who have passed easily.
- 4s – Echoseers: Pick up residual energy from where death occurred via photos, video, or location-based echoes.

Example overlaps:

• A Clairvoyant Bondreader Death Medium sees a story of what connects the dead with their sitter.

• A Clairsentient Veritant Death Medium feels a cold spot on their own chest that matches the wound that killed the spirit.

Channeler

Communicates with: Disincarnate spirits or intelligences

Role: The spirit speaks through the medium rather than to them. Channelers allow their body, voice, or energy field to be "ridden" or temporarily used by non-physical entities.

Clair dominant: Varies (usually Clairsentience or Claircognizance)

Key feature: The medium often remembers little or nothing of what was said

> "They aren't speaking to me. They use me to speak to you."

Best-suited archetypes:
- 7s – Lenseborns: Can deliver highly specific names, messages, or sounds exactly as they're channeled.
- 5s – Bondreaders: Usually connecting as the spirit wants to reconnect *because* of the bond with the sitter.
- 2s – Luminators: Channel aspirational beings that speak in encouragement, hope, or visionary potential.

Example overlaps:

• A Claircognizant Lenseborn Channeler delivers a list of names or precise prophecies with exact timestamps.

• A Clairsentient Veritant Channeler maintains clarity even while the entity speaks through them, knowing when to stop.

ORACLE

Communicates with: Deities or divine forces

Role: Acts as a conduit for messages from gods, goddesses, or divine beings. The Oracle is not limited to future messages. Gods may speak about truth, morality, cycles, or individual callings.

Clair dominant: Claircognizance, Clairvoyance, Clairaudience

Key feature: The message often has mythic weight or spiritual law

> "Oya warns: you're waging war where wisdom is needed."

Best-suited archetypes:
• 6s – Veritants: Naturally tuned to character truth, able to receive the essence of a deity or divine archetype.
• 2s – Luminators: See what is possible or destined in divine context, often deliver uplifting, purpose-driven messages.
• 3s – Harrowbinders: Oracles of shadow gods or death deities, revealing painful truths and initiatory experiences.

Example overlaps:

- A Clairvoyant Luminator Oracle sees a divine image of the sitter's highest potential with mythic clarity.
- A Clairaudient Harrowbinder Oracle hears Kanaloa describing a soul contract through whispered truths.

Prophet

Communicates with: Deities but only through precognition

Role: A type of Oracle who receives purely future-based messages from divine beings. The Prophet doesn't receive advice or commentary, only predictions.

Clair dominant: Claircognizance, Clairvoyance

Key feature: Future events delivered as divine warnings or decrees

> ***"The drought will last until the altar is rebuilt."***

Best-suited archetypes:
- 3s – Harrowbinders: Often mistake despair or future peril for prophecy, they may look like prophets but lack timeline specificity.
- 6s – Veritants: Deliver divine truths without distortion or emotional overlay, ideal for prophecy.
- 7s – Lenseborns: Can deliver exacting future details when the deity offers them specifics.

Example overlaps:

• A Claircognizant Veritant Prophet receives a flash of divine certainty: "There will be famine by spring."

• A Clairvoyant Lenseborn Prophet sees a war before it starts, down to military insignias and geographical coordinates.

Dark Medium

Communicates with: Monsters, mythological entities, and folkloric spirits (e.g., yokai, fae, tricksters, gods-as-creatures)

Role: Interacts with non-human intelligence rooted in cultural myth, fear, and folklore. They often walk the line between psychic explorers and supernatural negotiators. They are a zoologist but with entities.

Clair dominant: Clairvoyance, Clairsentience, Claircognizance

Key feature: Communication with beings that don't follow human morality or logic

> *"The thing in your attic isn't a ghost. It's a trickster. It wants attention, not peace."*

Best-suited archetypes:
- 3s – Harrowbinders: Naturally fearless and comfortable with the taboo; ideal for communication with mythic beasts, demons, or shadow entities.
- 4s – Echoseers: Perceive events and stories that the dark spirits or monsters need to convey.
- 1s – Lenseborns: Can track dark entities, the details about them, and what they need.

Example overlaps:
- A Clairaudient Harrowbinder Dark Medium hears the voice of a yokai that has haunted a family line.
- A Clairvoyant Echoseer Dark Medium can see a goblin running into the barn to hide.

Infernal Medium

Communicates with: Demons or infernal entities (based on theological or mythological systems)

Role: Speaks to beings associated with the underworld, damnation, or challenge. These mediums are not inherently evil but specialize in powerful, difficult, or morally complex spirits.

Clair dominant: Clairaudience, Clairvoyance

Key feature: Intensity. The messages may be confrontational, direct, or transformational.

> *"It's not trying to possess you. It's demanding acknowledgment of your rage."*

INFERNAL MEDIUM

Best-suited archetypes:

• 3s – Harrowbinders: Unflinching truth-seers, capable of handling morally gray or dangerous energies without judgment.

• 6s – Veritants: Capable of negotiating with infernal beings through exacting truth and moral clarity.

• 7s – Lenseborns: Provide precise names, sigils, contracts, or instructions from infernal communication.

Example overlaps:

• A Clairvoyant Harrowbinder Infernal Medium sees the weight of a demonic pact during a session.

• A Clairaudient Veritant Infernal Medium listens to what the entity wants and whether it's lying.

Celestial Medium

Communicates with: Angels, guides, or beings of divine light

Role: Works with entities associated with grace, healing, protection, and divine truth. These mediums often channel calm, high-frequency messages.

Clair dominant: Clairvoyance, Clairaudience, Claircognizance, Clairsentience

Key feature: Messages are uplifting, directive, or protective

> *"Your guide says you are protected, even in your delay."*

Best-suited archetypes:
- 2s – Luminators: Naturally tuned to divine love, inspiration, and messages of the highest potential.
- 6s – Veritants: Can accurately identify whether the "angel" is true or fabricated, and clarify the entity's purpose.
- 1s – Physicians: Work as healing channels with angelic or celestial beings for physical or spiritual restoration.

CELESTIAL MEDIUM

Example overlaps:

• A Clairvoyant Luminator Celestial Medium sees wings of light that uplift the sitter's destiny.

• A Clairaudient Physician Celestial Medium receives healing instructions directly from a celestial guide.

Pet/Animal Medium

Communicates with: Animals (living or deceased)

Role: Understands the thoughts, needs, and emotional experiences of animals. May work in healing, behavior, or grief support.

Clair dominant: Clairsentience, Clairalience, Claircognizance

Key feature: Direct communication about instinctual needs or companionship

> *"Your cat is upset because the litter box was moved closer to the noise."*

Best-suited archetypes:
- 1s – Physicians: Feel the well-being of animals and sense illness, injury, or emotional states.
- 5s – Bondreaders: Understand the energetic bonds between people and their animals, alive or passed.
- 4s – Echoseers: Sense the psychic "echo" of deceased pets or animal presences in videos and photos.

PET/ANIMAL MEDIUM

Example overlaps:

• A Clairsentient Bondreader Pet Medium feels the grief of a pet who passed when the leash is brought out.

• A Clairalient Physician Pet Medium smells where an animal is sick, even before diagnosis.

Plant Medium

Communicates with: Living plant spirits

Role: Listens to and interprets the consciousness or energetic needs of plant life. May receive messages about growth, land trauma, or herbal guidance.

Clair dominant: Clairsentience, Clairalience, Clairgustance, Claircognizance

Key feature: Green intelligence, connected to healing, earth balance, or plant memory

> ***"This willow is grieving. It misses the children."***

Best-suited archetypes:
- 1s – Physicians: Understand the health and vitality of plants, including trauma stored in the soil.
- 7s – Lenseborns: Perceive the energetic details of a plant.
- 4s – Echoseers: See the memory of what the land has witnessed, especially through trees or plant allies.

Example overlaps:
- A Clairalient Physician Plant Medium smells fungal rot in a tree whose roots were spiritually damaged.
- A Clairsentient Echoseer Plant Medium feels the loneliness of a neglected houseplant.

Weather Medium

Communicates with: Environmental and atmospheric forces

Role: Interprets and sometimes dialogues with natural forces like wind, storms, or drought. These mediums understand weather as a communicator, not just an event.

Clair dominant: Claircognizance, Clairsentience, Clairalience

Key feature: Weather changes respond to emotional or energetic truth

> *"The storm is not angry... it is correcting a long imbalance."*

Best-suited archetypes:
• 4s – Echoseers: Read shifting energy patterns in weather or environment with a wide-spanning psychic focus.
• 6s – Veritants: Interpret meaning behind environmental symbolism and truth in storm or calm.
• 1s – Physicians: See omens as it is in weather like rainbows, wind patterns, or sunlight as signals.

Example overlaps:
- A Clairsentient Echoseer Weather Medium feels storms as emotional maps of the collective unconscious.
- A Claircognizant Veritant Weather Medium knows the meaning of lightning that strikes during ritual.

Elemental Medium

Communicates with: Non-living objects or landforms as conscious entities (Animism)

Role: Understands the "soul" of rocks, buildings, tools, or locations. Speaks with the memory or spirit of inanimate things.

Clair dominant: Claircognizance, Clairvoyance, Clairsentient

Key feature: Everything has a story, even things we call lifeless

> *"This bridge doesn't want people on it anymore. It's tired. It held on longer than it should have."*

Best-suited archetypes:
- 5s – Bondreaders: Directly perceive the energetic cords between humans and "non-living" things, bridges, caves, tools, or ruins.
- 1s – Physicians: Can assess the wellness of a structure, stone, or path the same way they would a body.
- 4s – Echoseer: Discover the emotional pain or memory stored in weapons, land, or cursed objects.

Example overlaps:
- A Claircognizant Echoseer Elemental Medium touches a building and instantly knows it wants to be empty.
- A Clairsentient Harrowbinder Elemental Medium weeps when touching an axe used in a betrayal 200 years ago.

Putting It Together and Getting to Know the Author

As someone deeply embedded in the psychic world, my experiences transcend what many consider to be normal perception. My path, however, is not one of clear-cut boundaries between individual abilities but rather a complex and layered system of psychic faculties that often intersect and overlap in ways that make my experience unique and deeply interconnected. My abilities span across multiple layers of perception, from Over Sensitive Clairsentience to Clairvoyant and Claircognizant visions, and I work through various roles, including Dark Medium, Oracle, Infernal Medium, and Channeler.

The Over-Sensitive Clairsentient

The foundation of my psychic abilities rests in my Over Sensitive Clairsentience. As an OS Clairsentient, I experience emotions, energies, and physical sensations in overwhelming and consuming ways. Unlike a regular Clairsentient, who might merely feel a general emotional undertone or mild physical discomfort, I experience full-body sensations that may manifest as literal physical symptoms. These sensations are not my own. They are energetic imprints left behind by events, people, or locations that have significant emotional weight.

For example, when I walk into a space where someone has experienced trauma, I may physically feel the pain or discomfort they felt at that moment. My body can become flooded with sensations like sudden chest pressure, painful tightness in my throat, or even a deep stomach ache that mirrors the emotional turmoil or suffering that occurred there. These sensations come with no separation from my physical senses. They overpower them, overriding my own physical perception as I'm inundated with the energy of the past. In some cases, the energy may be so intense that it can trigger emotional responses. I can feel the grief, anger, or confusion that was once present, as if it's happening right now.

The complications? Stigmata. I have been hospitalized with a heart attack that I wasn't having, showing symptoms but not causation. I've had cuts or marks on my skin without any cause to make them happen. I have started bleeding without an incision. Simply, my body mimics the state of someone else's body without actually happening to me. I have felt a woman's pregnancy within myself (organs I don't have), and exposed her pregnancy by congratulating her... oops.

This makes me a powerful psychic, but the difference between me and others who identify as empaths is that I feel with precision, experiencing actual physical markers of someone else's emotional or energetic state. This connection is often deep, and it can lead to emotional overload or physical exhaustion if I'm not careful in managing these intense exchanges.

This is also why I'm a teacher for psychics. Because my body will reproduce what another psychic is going through, I can feel, analyze, and explain what is happening to them, pointing out things they may not even know to pay attention to.

Clairvoyant and Claircognizant Abilities

Alongside my Over Sensitive Clairsentience, my Clairvoyance and Claircognizance have become vital parts of my psychic experience. As a 9 Clairvoyant, my visions are dynamic and wide-reaching. My Clairvoyant abilities allow me to see broad impressions of events, people, and locations, like watching a cinematic experience unfold. I see events, creatures, and psychic imprints that tell me the story of what happened.

These visions are immersive and often come in theme-like forms, sometimes I see moving scenes, like a story playing out, while other times it is like watching a still image or snapshot from the past or future, almost all within my mind or slightly layered over the space I'm in.

As a 9 Claircognizant, my knowing comes through as instant insight into situations, people, or places. It is as if I know the truth of things the moment I come into contact with them. This knowledge is not intellectual or based on analysis; instead, it is a pure, deep understanding that arises intuitively and automatically. Whether I am meeting a new person or exploring a location, I just know things about the energy of that place or person, how they feel emotionally, the truth behind their words, or even the likely outcome of an event.

The Mediums: Dark, Infernal, Oracle, and Channeler

As someone who possesses a wide array of psychic *"gifts"* and roles, the most significant aspect of my experience comes from the mediumship realm. My work as a Dark Medium, Infernal Medium, Oracle, and Channeler creates a core foundation for much of my psychic interactions. These abilities allow me to connect with non-physical realms, whether it's speaking with spirits, receiving divine guidance, or connecting with entities of the underworld, demons, or mythological beings.

I see the creatures that go bump in the night, which is why my expertise is as an exorcist (See my book *Witchdoctor Exorcist*). I can also speak and understand the gods and their divine guidance as an oracle. As an OS Clairsentient, it is easy (although I don't allow it) for a spirit to jump in me and 'ride' me if they are lurking in this casual plane. And I know what the infernal have to say or their motivations.

Clairaudient Abilities

One crucial element of my mediumship is my ability to be Clairaudient when interacting with these beings. I am not Clairaudient with people. Meaning I can't hear someone's thoughts or the conversation details in another room. I can *know* them, but not actually hear them. Spirits? That's a different story. Through this ability, I can hear the voices of spirits and entities that speak directly to me. This allows me to receive messages and discern intentions through conversation. When I'm working as a Dark Medium, I connect with spirits and entities that are often considered outside traditional perceptions of life and death... beings that exist in shadowy realms, folklore, and the mythic unknown.

Dark Medium and Infernal Medium

The work of a Dark Medium and an Infernal Medium requires a great deal of sensitivity and psychic fortitude. These roles overlap, but each requires a different type of spiritual communication. Dark Mediums connect with beings from folklore, monsters, and entities that don't fit neatly into human understanding, such as kami, fae, and mythological creatures. These beings are often misunderstood and hold truths and messages that can help unlock deeper mysteries.

As a Dark Medium, my ability to hear these beings, especially with my Clairaudient skill, allows me to engage with spirits and creatures from the other side. They communicate with me in symbolic and direct ways, sometimes with threats, but often with warnings, teachings, or requests for intervention. I have developed the clarity and discernment to tell the difference between personal impressions and messages originating from the entities themselves.

Similarly, my work as an Infernal Medium involves communicating with demons or similar beings from faith-based frameworks. These energies are often viewed as dangerous or malevolent, but the truth is that they are messengers and catalysts for transformation. When I work with Infernal energies, I access the depth of human shadow, confronting the very fears and desires that we keep hidden. My ability to connect with these beings can offer insight into deep-rooted psychological or spiritual issues, often leading to profound personal revelations.

As a Channeler, I can become a vessel for a variety of spiritual entities, whether they are divine beings, demons, or ancestral spirits. These entities speak through me, using my voice, mind, and body to deliver messages to those in need. My ability to channel is not limited to human or earthly entities; I also channel beings of higher planes that can offer divine wisdom and guidance for those seeking clarity on their life path. Because these have major complications, I don't let them do this. The only time I allow a spirit to ride me is during healing sessions.

Harrowbinder: The Seeker of Hidden Truths

This is my best area. As a Harrowbinder, I act as an energy investigator, focusing on the shadows, the parts of people, and situations that they either hide or refuse to acknowledge. My OS Clairsentient abilities are particularly helpful in this regard, as I can feel the repressed emotions, fears, and traumas that people keep buried deep inside. As an OS Clairsentient Psychic, I physically experience the emotional weight of people, often feeling the sensation in my body, whether it's a tight chest, a feeling of suffocation, or nausea that accompanies emotional distress. This is why people hire me for missing persons' cases (things hidden) or to investigate people.

Combined with my Clairvoyant, Claircognizant, and Clairaudient skills, I can access emotional imprints and specific details related to the energy I am investigating. I "know" the story, even when no one else sees it, and this allows me to guide individuals through healing processes, helping them confront hidden fears and unspoken truths. This is especially useful in mediumship, where I can channel messages from the deceased or entities that help bring clarity and resolution to those still carrying these burdens.

Echoseer: The Witness to the Emotional Echoes

As an Echoseer, I can access events. My ability to perceive the echoes of events, people, and places is strong. With my Clairvoyant and Claircognizant abilities, I perceive these echoes as visual or intuitive impressions, but I am not focused on specific details; rather, I see the emotional atmosphere that lingers.

As a Claircognizant Echoseer, I "know" the story behind these imprints, whether it's a past trauma or a happy moment that has left an emotional mark. These imprints can often be felt through physical sensations, but my primary gift lies in my ability to read energy in an expansive way. I have developed the skill to interpret these imprints and use them as guidance, uncovering hidden truths or revealing past experiences that help inform present decisions.

Bondreader: The Keeper of Energetic Connections

As a Bondreader, I am highly attuned to the energy exchanges between people, places, and events. I can read the threads of energy that connect individuals or situations, allowing me to understand the dynamics at play. Whether these connections are healthy, frayed, damaged, or parasitic, my Claircognizant and Clairsentient abilities give me the ability to sense the flow of energy between beings. I can often feel how someone is energetically tied to another person, an event, or a situation, whether it's a positive or toxic connection.

As a Bondreader, I know how to track energy flows, understanding where the energy is stuck, broken, or draining. I work with clients to help them understand the energy dynamics in their relationships and give them the insight to shift or strengthen these connections as needed.

Lenseborn: The Seer of Precise Details

Finally, as a Lenseborn, my ability to perceive with laser-sharp focus allows me to hone in on specific details in the broad picture I'm often given. While my Clairvoyant and Clairsentient abilities are generally expansive, my Lenseborn ability allows me to zoom in on the details, such as the precise movements in a room, the exact objects in a location, or fine points that others may overlook. This is where my Clairvoyant and Claircognizant abilities come into play, helping me pinpoint important moments or missing details that others may not be able to access.

As a Lenseborn, my gifts extend to hyper-focused detail within the larger context of the energy I perceive. This makes me highly effective in crime scene investigations, past life regressions, and any work requiring attention to specific details in the energy field. I can hone in on these moments, understanding their importance and how they connect to larger patterns or narratives. This is great paired with being an Echoseer!

PUTTING IT TOGETHER AND GETTING TO KNOW...

I hope that you are able to figure out your own personalized profile based on all the information of the Seven Psychic Paths, to really understand yourself, as well as I understand you.

Warmly,
Aly Cardinalli
Your Psychic Witchdoctor

Aly Cardinalli

About the Author

Aly Cardinalli is an accomplished witchdoctor, performing arts specialist, psychic, and master educator with over twenty-five years of experience in his fields. He has dedicated his life to promoting traditional practices and spreading knowledge about culture.

ALY CARDINALLI

Born a dark medium and oversensitive psychic, Aly grew up surrounded by spirits and natural remedies that were used to cure both physical and spiritual ailments. He learned from various family members the art of healing, witchcraft, and spirituality, gradually developing a deep passion for indigenous and creolized practices.

As a young man, Aly decided to pursue a career in the performing arts. He studied music, dance, and theatrical directing, and quickly made a name for himself as a talented performer, exceptional choreographer (an expert in over eighteen styles of dance), and an award-winning director. His unique knowledge of the arts and culture, along with his exceptional stage presence, made him an instant hit with audiences across the globe, artistically directing/choreographing over 135 productions and performing in over 200.

Despite his success in the performing arts, Aly continued to practice traditional shamanic techniques. Aly has also developed an innovative training and classification system for psychics, mediums, and sensitives. Because of his genius and prodigy youth, his knowledge and aptitude in the inclusive disciplines of culture, healing, spirituality, mysticism, and storytelling are unmatched.

Over the years, Aly has gained immense popularity as a master educator in his fields. Aly has been the dean of education for a performing arts school, a teacher trainer, the headmaster at a witchcraft and psychic development school, and the education director for a healing arts institute.

Thanks to his dedication and hard work, Aly Cardinalli is now widely recognized as a commodity of cultural education. His talent, passion, and expertise have inspired countless people to embrace rich and vibrant culture and embrace the power of spiritual arts and ancient cultural expression.

Instagram/YouTube: @alycardinalli, tiktok @Aly.cardinalli

www.ingramcontent.com/pod-product-compliance
Lightning Source LLC
Chambersburg PA
CBHW071428150426
43191CB00008B/1079